# Inn-describably Delicious

## Recipes From The Illinois Bed & Breakfast Association Innkeepers



Tracy & Phyllis Winters

Winters Publishing
P.O. Box 501
Greensburg, Indiana 47240

(812) 663-4948

Printed in the United States of America

Cover photograph: By Teri Jones of Sweet Basil Hill Farm

The information about the inns and the recipes were supplied by the inns themselves. The rate information was current at the time of submission, but is subject to change. Every effort has been made to assure that the book is accurate. Neither the inns, authors, or publisher assume responsibility for any errors, whether typographical or otherwise.



Library of Congress Card Catalog Number 92-62532
ISBN 0-9625329-5-9

## Acknowledgements

We would like to thank the Illinois Bed & Breakfast
Association for working with us on this project,
and all of the innkeepers who took valuable time
to select recipes and fill out questionnaires.
Special thanks to Vickie Weger, Felicia Bucholtz
and Teri Jones for their help.
It is because of all of their efforts that we
were able to make this book a reality.

## Preface

Good cooking and hospitality have always gone "hand-in-hand." The same is true for Bed & Breakfasts and hospitality.

The Illinois Bed & Breakfast Association presents the following recipes for your enjoyment. Some are breakfast recipes, but you will also find many different types of recipes. Not all represent what you would actually be served at the listed Bed & Breakfasts (all B&B's are not allowed by their local governments to serve a full breakfast), but all do indicate the quality of hospitality you can expect. This cookbook introduces you to some of the finest inns in Illinois, where comfort and satisfaction are the goal.

Whether you are in search of the lightest muffin or the richest cheesecake, your tastebuds will not be disappointed. Take a look at the recipes in this book.

Then take a look at the Bed & Breakfasts represented. Whether you long for a bustling urban atmosphere or quiet walks along a country road, your desires can be met at an Illinois Bed & Breakfast Association Inn. Each Bed & Breakfast will be unique in style and personality, but you can count on cleanliness and hospitality - for that is our trademark.

No matter where you travel in Illinois, you can find a Bed & Breakfast nearby. Give us a call, partake of our hospitality, and let us serve you a wonderful breakfast.

In the meantime, enjoy fixing any of these recipes for yourself. Then take some time, get away, and visit us.

We're looking forward to seeing you,

The Illinois Bed & Breakfast Association (IBBA)

For more information about the IBBA or for a Guide of IBBA member B&B's, write:

The Illinois Bed & Breakfast Association
P.O. Box 823
Monmouth, IL 61462

# CONTENTS

# MUFFINS

# BACON-CHEDDAR MUFFINS

**1 3/4 cups flour**
**1/2 cup shredded sharp cheese (2 oz.)**
**1/4 cup sugar**
**2 teaspoons baking powder**
**1/4 teaspoon salt**
**1/4 teaspoon cayenne pepper**
**1 beaten egg**
**3/4 cup milk**
**1/3 cup cooking oil**
**1/3 cup (6 strips) bacon, cooked crisp & drained**

Mix dry ingredients together. Mix egg, milk, and shortening together and add to flour mixture all at once. Stir until moist. Batter will be lumpy. Fry bacon until crisp, drain and crumble, fold into batter. Grease cups and top of muffin pan and fill cups to the top. Makes 8 large muffins.

---

Submitted by:

Seacord House B&B
624 N. Cherry St.
Galesburg, IL 61401
(309) 342-4107
Gwen & Lyle Johnson
$35.00 to $40.00

Continental plus breakfast
3 rooms
Children, over 12
No pets
No smoking
Mastercard & Visa

1890's landmark house, furnished in Victorian decor with family antiques. Freshly-made muffins or waffles are daily specialties. Arrangements can be made for special occasions. Close to Knox College, Carl Sandburg's birthplace, Bishop Hill, Spoon River country. Your schedule accommodated.

# FRESH APPLE MUFFINS

**4 cups diced apples (peeled or unpeeled)**
**1 cup sugar**
**1 cup whole wheat flour**
**1 cup all-purpose flour**
**2 teaspoons baking soda**
**2 teaspoons cinnamon**
**1 teaspoon salt**
**1 cup broken walnuts (leave in large pieces)**
**2 eggs, beaten lightly**
**1/2 cup oil**
**2 teaspoons vanilla extract**
**1 cup raisins**

Mix apples and sugar. Mix dry ingredients, including nuts. Now mix eggs, oil and vanilla. Add to apples and sugar. Add raisins to wet mixture, and mix thoroughly. Sprinkle dry flour mixture over the apple mixture. Spoon into greased muffin tins. Bake at 325° for 25 minutes. Serve warm.

---

Submitted by:

Bishop's Inn Bed & Breakfast
223 W. Central Blvd.
Kewanee, IL 61443
(309) 852-5201
Terriska Urban
$55.00 to $85.00

Full breakfast
4 rooms, 4 private baths
Children, over 12
Pets allowed
Restricted smoking

Stately Victorian home, formerly a rectory, offers a/c suites. Lovely antique furnishings, stained glass windows, oak floors. Romantic yard with perennial flower beds, brick walkways, gazebo, heart-shaped rose arbor. Warm hospitality. We use fresh herbs grown in our kitchen garden.

# MANDARIN ORANGE MUFFINS

**2 cups all-purpose flour**
**2 tablespoons sugar**
**1 tablespoon baking powder**
**1/2 teaspoon salt**
**1 egg**
**1/2 cup milk**
**1/4 cup salad oil**
**1/4 cup orange juice**
**6 oz. can mandarin oranges, drained**

Preheat oven to 400°. Mix all dry ingredients with a fork in large bowl. Beat egg slightly in small bowl, add milk, salad oil, and orange juice. Add egg mixture to flour all at once. Mix until flour is moistened. Crush mandarin oranges with a fork, and add to batter mixture. Divide mixture into 12 individual greased muffin tins. Bake 20 - 25 minutes. Muffins should be well-risen and golden brown. Serve immediately. Makes 12 muffins.

---

Submitted by:

The Brick House
Bed & Breakfast
Box 301 - Conklin Ct.
Goodfield, IL 61742
(800) 322-2304
Chaunce Conklin
$50.00 to $60.00 (B&B only)
$80.00 to $110.00 (B&B/
Dinner Theatre pkg.)

Full breakfast
4 rooms
No children
No pets
No smoking

Beautiful old home transports you back through history to it's 1857 origins, and the bold, pioneer spirit so special to the Illinois heartland in the pre-Civil War era when Abe Lincoln traveled the historic Heritage Trail. Experience professional dinner theatre located behind the Brick House. A great overnight package!

# MAPLE BRAN MUFFINS

**3/4 cup natural wheat bran**
**1/2 cup milk**
**1/2 cup maple syrup**
**1 egg, slightly beaten**
**1/4 cup oil**
**1 1/4 cups whole wheat flour**
**3 teaspoons baking powder**
**1/2 teaspoon salt**
**1/3 cup chopped walnuts**

**Glaze:**
**1 tablespoon butter**
**1 tablespoon maple syrup**
**1/2 cup confectioner's sugar**

Combine bran, milk, and maple syrup. Mix in egg and oil. Combine remaining muffin ingredients separately. Add bran mixture, stirring until just moistened. Divide batter into 12 greased muffin tins. Bake at 400° for 18 - 20 minutes. Combine glaze ingredients, stirring to blend, and spread over warm muffins. Makes 12 muffins.

---

Submitted by:

Linda's Country Loft
R.R. #1, Box 198A
Monticello, IL 61856
(217) 762-7316
Linda Howarter
$40.00 to $55.00

Continental plus breakfast
3 rooms, 1 private bath
Children allowed
No pets
No smoking

Guests enjoy a 15 year old home in a peaceful, wooded setting overlooking the Sangamon River, minutes away from University of IL, and seasonal attractions. Homemade breakfast will be served in formal dining room on fine china, or on screened-in porch, weather permitting.

# SUGARLESS FRUIT MUFFINS

**2 cups unbleached flour (or 1 1/2 cups white & 1/2 cup whole wheat)**
**1/2 teaspoon baking soda**
**2 teaspoons baking powder**
**1/2 cup nuts**
**1/2 teaspoon nutmeg**
**1/2 teaspoon cinnamon**
**1/2 cup chopped golden raisins**
**2 tablespoons grated orange or lemon zest**
**2 tablespoons frozen apple or orange juice concentrate**
**1/4 cup canola or olive oil**
**2 egg whites or 1 egg**
**1 1/4 cups pureed fruit (bananas, apples, berries, pumpkin, etc.)**

In food processor bowl combine dry ingredients, raisins and orange or lemon zest. Process until raisins and zest are chopped. Set aside. In food processor, puree fruit (if using berries, use directly from freezer), add rest of liquid ingredients, blend. Add dry ingredients and nuts. Use on/off to blend or blend by hand as for any muffins. Preheat oven to 400°. Spray 12 cup muffin pan with nonstick coating. Fill cups evenly and bake 17 - 18 minutes. Remove from pan and serve warm or cool and freeze. Recipe freezes well. May be doubled. If frozen, remove from freezer 3 - 4 hours before serving or night before. To heat place on cookie sheet, and heat in 300° oven 10 - 15 minutes. Makes 12 muffins.

---

Submitted by:

Maggie's Bed & Breakfast
2102 N. Keebler
Collinsville, IL 62234
(618) 344-8283
Maggie Leyda
$35.00 to $65.00

Full breakfast
5 rooms, 4 private baths
Children allowed
Pets allowed
Smoking allowed

Beautiful, quiet, country setting just minutes from downtown St. Louis. Near hospital, restaurants, & shopping. Cooking with natural ingredients. Antiques and art objects collected in world-wide travels. Games, cable TV, and hot tub with terrycloth robes & houseslippers.

# FRENCH TOAST, PANCAKES & WAFFLES

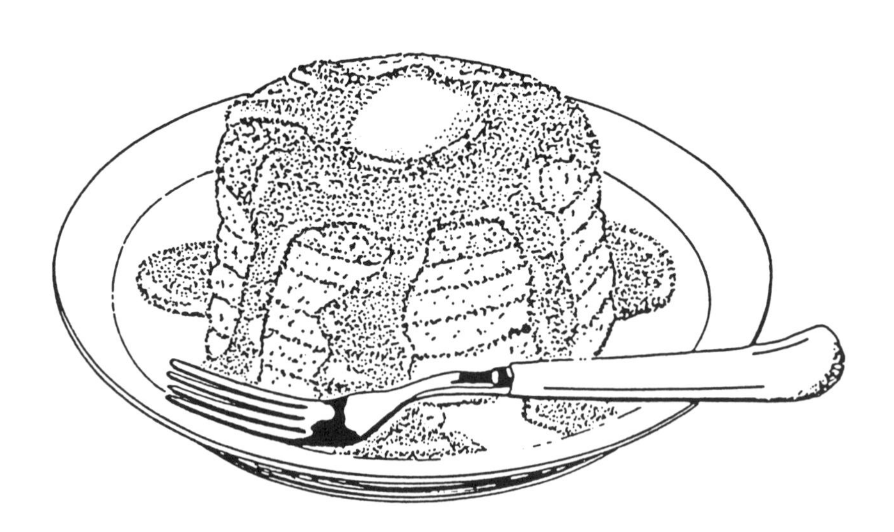

# APPLESAUCE PANCAKES

**2 cups pancake mix**
**1 1/4 cups milk**
**1 egg**
**2 tablespoons melted shortening or oil**
**1/4 teaspoon cinnamon**
**1/4 - 1/2 cup applesauce**
**1/8 cup ground walnuts or pecans**

Using your favorite pancake mix, beat mix, milk, egg, shortening, and cinnamon until blended. Add 1/4 - 1/2 cup applesauce to desired consistency; add ground nutmeats. Makes 15 pancakes. Enjoy!

---

Submitted by:

Lord Stocking's
Bed & Breakfast
803 Third Avenue
Mendota, IL 61342
(815) 539-7905
Lee Stocking
$35.00 to $100.00

Continental breakfast
5 rooms, 1 private bath,
1 1/2 shared baths
Children, over 10
Pets allowed
No smoking

This 16-room Victorian home has well-tended lawns with an English garden. Home is air-conditioned and rooms are furnished with antiques. Accommodations include a 2-room suite with private bath and balcony.

# CHOCOLATE WAFFLES WITH CINNAMON BUTTER

**Waffles:**
**2/3 cup all-purpose flour**
**1/2 teaspoon baking powder**
**1/4 teaspoon salt**
**1/3 cup sugar**
**1 1/2 tablespoons cocoa**
**2 eggs, separated**
**1/4 cup commercial sour cream**
**3 tablespoons butter or margarine, melted**
**1/8 teaspoon cream of tartar**

**Cinnamon Butter:**
**1/2 cup unsalted butter or margarine, softened**
**1 tablespoon honey**
**1/2 teaspoon ground cinnamon**

Combine first 5 waffle ingredients, set aside. Combine egg yolks, sour cream, and butter. Add to flour mixture, stirring until blended. Beat egg whites (at room temperature) and cream of tartar until stiff peaks form. Carefully fold whites into batter. Bake in preheated, oiled waffle iron. Beat Cinnamon Butter ingredients together well. Serve with waffles. Makes 6 - 4" waffles and 1/2 cup of butter.

---

Submitted by:

Country Palmer House
R.R. #3, Box 254
Mt. Carroll, IL 61053
(815) 244-2343
Allan & JoAnn Palmer
$40.00 to $75.00

Full breakfast
4 rooms, 2 private baths
Children allowed
No pets
No smoking
Mastercard & Visa

1911 remodeled farm home - fireplace in family room. Quiet, with beautiful view from top of ridge in northwest Ilinois. Furnished with many oak antique pieces. Farm tours available. Hayrides and bonfires can be arranged on premises. Country breakfast.

# CINNAMON-APPLE FRENCH TOAST

**8 tart apples**
**8 tablespoons brown sugar**
**1 teaspoon cinnamon**
**8 pats of butter**
**6 eggs**
**1/2 cup milk**
**1/2 teaspoon vanilla**
**16 slices thick bread (Texas toast is good)**

Peel and core apples. Cut into slices as for a pie. Mix brown sugar and cinnamon in large bowl. Add apple slices and mix thoroughly. Separate into 8 microwave safe bowls. Put a pat of butter on each helping. Beat eggs, milk, and vanilla in a bowl. Dip slices of bread and fry on a hot greased griddle. Microwave apples until butter melts. Serve toast & cinnamon apples on warmed plates. Makes 8 servings.

---

Submitted by:

Belle Aire Guest House
11410 Route 20 West
Galena, IL 61036
(815) 777-0893
Jan & Lorraine Svec
$65.00 to $85.00

Full breakfast
4 rooms, 4 private baths
Children allowed
No pets
No smoking
Mastercard, Visa, Discover

1836 Federal-style home on 16 acres with a tamarack lined driveway. Just 3 minutes from downtown Galena, but surrounded by the quiet of the countryside. We love welcoming guests into our home. Come visit!

# CREAMY PEACH-FILLED FRENCH TOAST

**3 oz. pkg. cream cheese, softened**
**1/2 cup chopped peaches**
**2 tablespoons chopped pecans**
**1 tablespoon honey**
**6 - 8 slices French bread, cut diagonally 1 1/2" thick**
**2 eggs**
**1/2 cup half & half**
**1/4 teaspoon vanilla**

In small bowl, beat cream cheese until light. Add peaches, nuts, and honey. Cut pocket in each slice of bread. Carefully fill each with 1 1/2 tablespoons of cheese mixture. Heat griddle to 350°. In shallow bowl, slightly beat eggs. Add half & half, and vanilla. Lightly grease griddle. Dip bread in egg mixture. Coat both sides. Cook 3 - 4 minutes on each side. Serve with syrup, butter, or sliced fresh fruit. Makes 4 servings.

---

Submitted by:

Aunt Zelma's Country Guest Home
1074 County Road 800 North
Tolono, IL 61880
(217) 485-5101
Zelma Weibel
$40.00 to $45.00

Full breakfast
3 rooms, 1 private bath
Children allowed
No pets
No smoking

This one-story country home is furnished with family antiques and quilts. It is near Champaign, and the University of Illinois, and just three miles from Willard Airport.

# CRUMB-TOPPED BAKED FRENCH TOAST

**French Toast:**
**2 eggs, well-beaten**
**1/2 cup milk**
**1/2 teaspoon salt**
**1/2 teaspoon vanilla**
**6 slices thick-sliced bread**
**1 cup Corn Flake crumbs**
**1/4 cup melted butter**

**Cinnamon Syrup:**
**1 1/3 cups sugar**
**1/3 cup water**
**2/3 cup white corn syrup**
**1 teaspoon ground cinnamon**
**5 oz. can Milnot**
**1/2 teaspoon almond flavoring**
**1/2 teaspoon burnt sugar flavoring (opt.)**
**1 tablespoon butter**

Combine eggs, milk, salt and vanilla, mix well. Dip bread slices into egg mixture. Coat both sides with crumbs. Place on well-greased cookie sheet. Drizzle with melted butter. Bake 10 minutes at 450°. Makes 3 - 4 servings. Serve with Cinnamon Syrup: Combine sugar, water, corn syrup, and cinnamon in saucepan. Bring to a boil, cook 2 minutes. Remove from heat, add Milnot, flavorings, and butter. Serve warm over toast.

---

Submitted by:

The Goddard Place
R.R. 2, Box 445G
Anna, IL 62906
(618) 833-6256
Jim & Edna Goddard
$30.00 to $40.00

Full breakfast
3 rooms
Children, over 5
No pets
Restricted smoking
Mastercard & Visa

Beautiful country setting, with a peaceful atmosphere. Large pond, loaded with nice sized catfish and bass, is only 40 yards from the back door. Sit and relax, or read, on the huge deck, or in the Great Room with its stone fireplace.

# FRENCH TOAST WITH ALMOND FLAVOR

**6 slices homemade bread**
**1/4 cup milk**
**2 eggs, beaten**
**1/2 teaspoon almond extract**
**2 tablespoons butter or margarine**
**Sifted powdered sugar**

Combine milk, eggs, and almond extract in a shallow dish; stir well. Dip bread slices into egg mixture, turning to coat both sides. Melt 1 tablespoon butter in large skillet. Arrange bread slices in skillet, and cook over medium heat until golden. Transfer to serving plate, and keep warm until ready to serve. Sprinkle French toast with powdered sugar and serve. If you wish, serve with almond flavored butter. Makes 2 servings.

---

Submitted by:

The Hill House
503 S. Locust
Sesser, IL 62884
(618) 625-6064
Dewey and Gwen Nussbaum
$45.00 to $50.00

Continental plus breakfast
3 rooms, 3 private baths
Children allowed
No pets
Restricted smoking
Mastercard & Visa

Built in 1914 by James H. Hill for his family home. Hill also built the historical Opera House, as well as most of the buildings on Franklin Avenue. The house is stucco at the top, and it's interior has had few changes; several original light fixtures remain in use today. Abe Lincoln slept in one of the beds on a visit to southern Illinois.

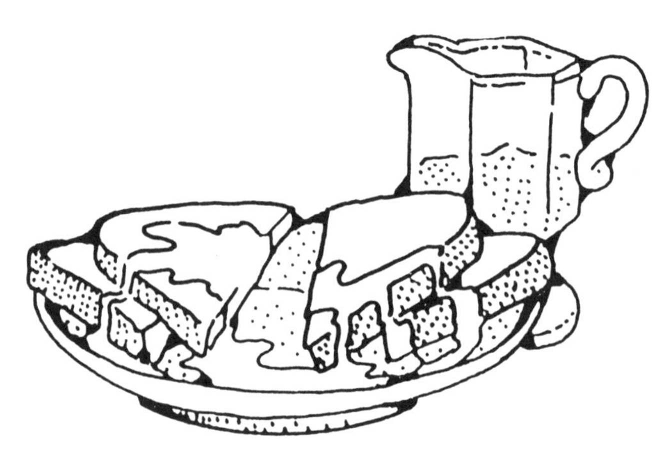

# GINGERBREAD WAFFLES

**1/2 cup shortening**
**1/4 cup packed brown sugar**
**1 egg**
**1/2 cup light molasses**
**1 1/2 cups all-purpose flour**
**3/4 teaspoon ground ginger**
**3/4 teaspoon ground cinnamon**
**1/2 teaspoon baking powder**
**1/2 teaspoon baking soda**
**1/2 teaspoon salt**
**1/2 cup boiling water**

Lightly grease and preheat waffle baker. Cream shortening and brown sugar until light. Add egg and molasses, beat well. Stir together flour, spices, baking powder, soda, and salt. Add to creamed mixture alternately with 1/2 cup boiling water, beating after each addition. Pour approximately 1/3 of batter into preheated baker. Close lid quickly, do not open during baking. Remove waffle from baker with a fork. Serve with heated fruit, preserves, sauce or powdered sugar. If served as a dessert, you may top with Cool Whip, ice cream, pudding, or lemon sauce. Waffles may be made ahead and frozen. Reheat in toaster or oven. Very versatile and delicious! Makes approximately 4 waffles.

---

Submitted by:

Harshbarger Homestead
R.R. #1, Box 110
Atwood, IL 61913
(217) 578-2265
Dale & Shirley Harshbarger
$35.00 to $45.00 Family rates
(Children - $10.00)

Continental plus breakfast
3 rooms
Children allowed
No pets
Restricted smoking

Comfortable country home built in 1914, with many antiques and collectibles. Large playroom with children's sleeping quarters. Herb & flower garden, organic, & Oriental vegetable gardens. Bird lovers' delight. 150 year old rebuilt log cabin. Near Amish community.

# OVERNIGHT CARAMEL TOAST

**1 cup brown sugar**
**1/2 cup butter**
**2 tablespoons white corn syrup**
**12 slices bread**
**6 eggs, beaten**
**1 1/2 cups milk**
**1 teaspoon vanilla**
**1/4 teaspoon salt**

In saucepan, combine brown sugar, butter and corn syrup. Heat slowly and stir constantly as it cooks, until thickened. Spread evenly in 9" x 13" pan. Mix eggs, milk, vanilla, and salt well. Dip 6 slices of bread and place over caramel mixture. Dip 6 more and place over the first six. Pour remaining batter evenly over bread. Cover and chill 8 hours or overnight. Bake at 350° for 35 - 40 minutes, or until evenly browned. Makes 4 servings.

---

Submitted by:

Mississippi Memories
R.R. #1, Box 291
Nauvoo, IL 62354
(217) 453-2771
Marge & Dean Starr
$45.00 to $65.00

Full breakfast
4 rooms, 2 private baths
No pets
No smoking
No alcohol
Mastercard & Visa

Spacious home in quiet, wooded setting on Mississippi River. Enjoy spectacular sunsets, moonlit nights, barges drifting by, and wildlife-watching from 2 decks. Elegantly served breakfast. Fruit and flowers in rooms, 2 fireplaces, piano, a/c. 5 minutes to restored Mormon city of Nauvoo. Geode hunting.

# TAHITIAN FRENCH TOAST

**8 oz. pkg. cream cheese**
**1 cup crushed pineapple**
**1 cup chopped pecans**
**1 lb. loaf French bread**
**4 eggs**
**1 cup heavy whipping cream**
**1 teaspoon vanilla**

**Syrup:**
**1 - 12 oz. jar apricot jam**
**1/2 cup orange juice**

Beat cream cheese and pineapple together. Add pecans and set aside. Cut French bread into 1 1/4" slices. Cut a pocket in the top of each and fill with approximately 1 - 2 tablespoons of cream cheese mixture. Beat eggs well; add heavy cream and vanilla. Dip bread in egg mixture and cook on lightly greased griddle. Heat jam and orange juice; drizzle on top of toast. Makes 8 - 10 servings.

---

Submitted by:

Carmody's Clare Inn
207 South 12 Street
Petersburg, IL 62675
(217) 632-2350
Pat & Mike Carmody
$40.00 (sgl.) to $50.00 (dbl.)

Full breakfast
3 rooms
Children, over 10
No pets
No smoking

Built in 1874, and lovingly restored, with its ceiling medallions, marble mantels, and hand-grained woodwork gloriously intact. Antique furnishings recreate the ambience of yesteryear. Near golf & tennis, and New Salem, where Abe Lincoln wooed Ann Rutledge. Lincoln's home, law office & tomb are just a few miles further in Springfield.

# WHITNEY PANCAKE

**2 cups Bisquick**
**1 teaspoon cinnamon**
**1 cup milk**
**2 eggs**
**1/2 cup walnuts**
**1/2 cup raisins**
**1 1/2 cups chopped apples**
**12 brown-n-serve sausages**

**Cider Sauce:**
**1 cup sugar**
**3 tablespoons Bisquick**
**1/4 teaspoon cinnamon**
**1/4 cup butter**
**2 cups real apple cider**

For pancake: Mix 2 cups Bisquick, 1 teaspoon cinnamon, 1 cup milk and 2 eggs. Add walnuts, raisins and chopped apples. Put into greased 9" x 13" pan. Bake at 400° - 425° for 20 - 25 minutes. Before baking pancake lay 12 brown-n-serve sausages on top. Serve with Cider Sauce. For sauce: Heat all ingredients until thick. Serve with warm pancake. Makes 6 servings.

---

Submitted by:

The Whitney
1620 Whitney Rd.
Franklin Grove, IL
61031
(815) 456-2526
Sheryl Lyons
$50.00 plus tax

Full breakfast
6 rooms, 3 1/2 private baths
Children allowed (babies in same room, older children pay extra for room)
No pets
No smoking

Built in 1856 by Col. Nathan Whitney, on the National Register of Historic Places, and is home of the Whitney #20 Crab Apple. Special features are feather beds, large old-fashioned bath tubs and antique furnishings.

# EGG, MEAT & CHEESE DISHES

# BAKED EGG CASSEROLE

**1/2 lb. French bread, trimmed & cubed**
**2 lbs. pork sausage, browned & drained**
**16 eggs, beaten**
**1 1/2 cups grated medium sharp cheese**

Grease 9" x 13" casserole and put bread cubes in the bottom. Brown and drain sausage. Place on top of the bread. Beat eggs well and pour over the top. Add cheese. Cover with foil and refrigerate overnight. Bake at 350° for 30 - 35 minutes.

---

Submitted by:

Nostalgia Corner
115 W. Seventh
Beardstown, IL 62618
(217) 323-5382
Doug & Diana Webb
$45.00

Full breakfast
5 rooms, 3 private baths
Children allowed, with advance arrangements
No pets
Restricted smoking

The Webb House B&B with Front Porch gifts and Coach House Blacksmith steps you into the nostalgic feelings of 19th century charm & hospitality. Filled with antiques and old-fashioned caring. Enjoy our laughing fire, library, music room, TV, ping-pong, checkers, and other games for your leisure.

# CHILI-EGG PUFF

**10 eggs**
**1/2 cup flour**
**1 teaspoon baking powder**
**1/2 teaspoon salt**
**8 oz. Cheddar cheese, shredded**
**16 oz. small curd cottage cheese**
**1/2 cup melted butter**
**2 - 4 oz. cans diced chilies**

Beat eggs until light and lemon colored. Add flour, baking powder, salt, cheeses and melted butter. Blend. Stir in chilies. Pour into well-buttered pan and bake at 350° for 35 minutes or until browned and firm. Makes 10 - 12 servings.

---

Submitted by:

Top O' The Morning
1505 19th Ave.
Rock Island, IL 61201
(309) 786-3513
Sam & Peggy Doak
$40.00 to $60.00

Full breakfast
3 rooms, 3 private baths
Children allowed
No pets
Restricted smoking

Prairie style brick home with slate roof, copper guttering and large copper canopy over front entrance. Spectacular view of Quad Cities and Mississippi River from screened porch or deck. Wrought iron fence and gates define entrance to 3 acres of oak and fruit trees, vegetable garden, and fountain in the circle drive.

# CRUSTLESS QUICHE

**5 eggs, beaten**
**12 oz. frozen hash brown potatoes, unthawed**
**1 chopped onion**
**1/2 cup cottage cheese**
**1 cup grated cheese**
**1/4 teaspoon salt**
**1/8 teaspoon pepper**
**Dash of hot pepper sauce**
**Paprika to taste**
**6 - 8 slices bacon, cooked & crumbled**

Combine all ingredients except paprika and bacon. Pour into 9" - 10" pie plate. Sprinkle with paprika. Bake at 350° for 25 minutes, until set. Sprinkle with bacon. Bake 5 minutes more. Let stand 5 minutes before serving. This recipe can be made the night before, and refrigerated. Makes 5 - 6 servings.

---

Submitted by:

Phyllis's Bed & Breakfast
801 Ninth Street
Highland, IL 62249
(618) 654-4619
Bob & Phyllis Bible
$40.00 to $55.00

Full breakfast
4 rooms, 4 private baths
Children, over 12
No pets
No smoking
Mastercard & Visa

100 year old inn in busy little town of 7,500. 25 minutes from St. Louis. Gift shop. Walk to town square and restaurants. Breakfast served on deck, weather permitting. Near tennis, swimming, and golf. Fireplace burning in winter.

# "EGG AND CHEESE THING"

**12 eggs, beaten**
**12 slices bread, buttered & cubed**
**1 lb. Velveeta cheese, cubed**
**4 cups milk**
**1/4 teaspoon dry mustard**
**Salt & pepper to taste**
**Ham cubes, bacon, onions, etc., as desired**

Mix together eggs, bread cubes, cheese, milk, and seasonings. Add ham cubes, crisply cooked bacon, onions, or whatever other fillings you may like. Place in large oven-proof bowl, large enough to fill only 2/3 full, as mixture puffs while baking. Place in refrigerator overnight. Bake at 350° for one hour and 15 minutes, or until set. Makes 6 - 8 servings.

---

Submitted by:

Happy Wanderer Inn B&B
309 Collinsville Ave.
Collinsville, IL 62234
(618) 344-0477
Yvonne Holst
$35.00 to $60.00

Continental plus breakfast
4 rooms, 2 shared baths
Children, over 3
No pets
Restricted smoking

Built in 1889, by the Lithuanian people as a parsonage for the quaint Lutheran church next door. Large spacious rooms, split foyer, winding staircase. Filled with antiques. Front porch with swing. Sitting room for lounging, with cable TV, board games, newspapers. 10 miles from St. Louis.

# GRITS CASSEROLE

**4 cups water**
**1 teaspoon salt**
**1 cup quick-cooking grits**
**4 eggs, lightly beaten**
**1 lb. pork sausage, browned & drained**
**1 1/2 cups shredded sharp Cheddar cheese, divided**
**1/2 cup milk**
**1/4 cup butter, softened**

In saucepan, bring water and salt to a boil. Slowly stir in grits. Reduce heat and cook 4 - 5 minutes, stirring occasionally. Remove grits from heat and add a small amount of hot grits to the eggs. Return to saucepan. Stir in browned and drained sausage, 1 cup cheese, milk and butter. Stir until the butter melts. Pour into greased 9" x 13" pan. Sprinkle with remaining cheese. Bake at 350° for 50 minutes or until the top begins to brown. (Leftover portions are even tasty served cold.) Makes 10 - 12 servings.

---

Submitted by:

Dicus House Bed & Breakfast
609 E. Broadway St.
Streator, IL 61634
(815) 672-6700
Felicia & Art Bucholtz
$45.00 to $55.00

Full breakfast
4 rooms, 3 private baths
Children, over 10
No pets
No smoking
Mastercard & Visa

Situated near 3 state parks, this historic 1890 home welcomes you to a bygone era. 6 marble fireplaces, carved walnut woodwork, and original brick walks, all in a park-like setting. Buffet breakfast in formal dining room. Lunch & dinner by advance request. Evening snacks.

# HAM, EGGS, AND ONIONS

**1 medium onion, sliced**
**8 oz. ham, cubed (not the cooked and canned type)**
**8 eggs, beaten**
**1/4 cup milk**
**1 tablespoon butter (for skillet)**

Brush skillet with butter. Slice onion and sauté for 5 minutes, covered. Add ham cubes. Stir and cook for 5 minutes. Add eggs beaten with milk, and "scramble" until soft-cooked, not browned. Makes 6 servings.

---

Submitted by:

The Ancient Pines
2015 Parley St.
Nauvoo, IL 62354
(217) 453-2767
Genevieve Simmens
$35.00 to $39.00

Full breakfast
3 rooms
Children allowed
Pets, outdoors only
Restricted smoking

Brick Victorian, stained glass windows, etched glass door, pressed tin and copper ceilings. 140 year old evergreens, homemade bread. 30 restored homes in Mormon area. Icarian Museum, Indian artifacts, winery.

# HARVEST CASSEROLE

**2 lbs. bulk pork sausage**
**2 apples, cored & sliced**
**9 slices bread, crusts removed and cut into cubes**
**3/4 teaspoon dry mustard**
**9 eggs, beaten**
**1 1/2 cups grated sharp Cheddar cheese**
**3 cups milk**

Fry the sausage in a skillet, breaking it up as it cooks, drain on paper towels. Reserve the fat. Place sausage in lightly greased 9" x 13" x 2" baking dish, or divide between two 1 1/2 quart casseroles. Sauté apple slices in sausage fat. Combine apples, bread cubes, mustard, eggs, cheese and milk, and mix well. Pour this mixture over sausage. Cover and refrigerate overnight. Heat oven to 350°. Bake covered for 30 minutes. Uncover and bake another 30 minutes. Makes 12 servings.

---

Submitted by:

The Carr Mansion
Guest House
416 East Broadway
Monmouth, IL 61642
(309) 734-3654
Christopher & Carla Kanthak
$40.00

Full breakfast
3 rooms
Children, over 12
No pets
No smoking
Mastercard & Visa

3 story, 20 room mansion, built in 1877. On National Register, with many of the original fixtures, unique architectural features, and cozy nooks for relaxing and reflection. Warm weather guests may enjoy veranda or balcony. In winter, drawing room or library are popular retreats. 3 blocks from city square with restaurants and shopping.

# MAY MEMORIES BREAKFAST

**1 lb. asparagus, cut into 1" pieces**
**1 lb. bulk sausage**
**1 1/2 cups milk**
**2 chicken bouillon cubes**
**10 1/2 oz. can cream of mushroom soup**
**8 slices toast**
**2 hard-boiled eggs, sliced**
**Accompaniments:**
**1 pint strawberries**
**8 oz. carton blueberry yogurt**

In large saucepan over medium-high heat, boil the asparagus in 1/2" of water for 8 minutes. Set aside. In large skillet, crumble and brown sausage. Drain off grease. Add the milk and bouillon cubes, and simmer until bouillon is dissolved. Add the mushroom soup, stirring often until heated through. Add asparagus. Arrange 2 slices of toast on each of 4 serving plates. Spoon the sausage mixture over the toast, and arrange sliced egg on the top. Place strawberries in dessert dishes, and spoon a dollop of yogurt over each serving. Serves 4.

---

Submitted by:

Yesterdays Memories
303 E. Peru St.
Princeton, IL 61356
(815) 872-7753
Marilyn & Robert Haslam
$40.00

Full breakfast
2 rooms
Children allowed, by special arrangement only
No pets
No smoking

An 1850's home, located in historic Princeton, one of Illinois' best antiquing spots. Furnished in country antiques. Owners are interested in architectural restoration, mechanical musical instruments, organic gardening, and miniatures.

# MEAT AND CHEESE STRATA

**3 1/2 cups French bread cut into 3/4" cubes**
**12 oz. brown-n-serve sausage**
**1 cup chopped fresh tomatoes, divided**
**1/2 cup chives**
**1 cup shredded mild Cheddar cheese, divided**
**4 eggs**
**12 oz. can undiluted evaporated milk**
**3 tablespoons all-purpose flour**
**1 teaspoon dry mustard**
**3/4 teaspoon Cavender's Greek seasoning**

Lay out bread cubes on baking sheet. Bake at 350° for approximately 8 minutes or until dry. Lightly grease 12" x 7" x 2" baking dish. Layer half of the bread cubes, sausage, tomatoes, chives and cheese. Repeat layers. In mixing bowl, combine eggs, evaporated milk, flour, mustard, and seasoning; blend well. Pour egg mixture over bread mixture, pressing down to saturate all the bread. Bake in preheated 350° oven for 40 minutes, or until puffed and custard is set. Let stand 10 minutes before serving. Makes 6 servings.

---

Submitted by:

Green Tree Inn
15 Mill St., P.O. Box 96
Elsah, IL 62035
(618) 374-2821
Michael & Mary Ann Pitchford
$65.00 to $90.00

Full breakfast
9 rooms, 9 private baths
Children, over 12
No pets
No smoking
Mastercard, Visa, Discover

Circa 1850-style inn: Federal, Victorian and country rooms. Located in heart of historic Elsah, the "New England of the Midwest." Balcony off each room. Gathering room for fireside chats. Attractive, scrumptious breakfasts. Also available for private business lunches or receptions.

# MEAT AND POTATO QUICHE

- **3 tablespoons vegetable oil**
- **3 cups raw shredded potatoes**
- **1 cup grated cheese**
- **3/4 cup cooked chicken or diced ham or browned hamburger**
- **1/4 cup chopped onion**
- **1 cup rich milk**
- **5 eggs**
- **1/2 teaspoon salt**
- **1/8 teaspoon pepper**
- **1 tablespoon parsley flakes**

Mix the oil and potatoes in large pie pan and press evenly into pie crust shape. Bake at 425° for 15 minutes, until beginning to brown. Layer the cheese, meat and onion. In bowl, beat together milk, eggs, salt and pepper. Pour over other ingredients and sprinkle with parsley flakes. Bake 30 minutes at 425°. Makes 6+ servings.

---

Submitted by:

Prairie Path Guest House
R.R. #3, Box 223
Mt. Carroll, IL 61053
(815) 244-3462
DeLos & Fern Stadel
$50.00 to $60.00

Full breakfast
3 rooms, 1 private bath
No children
No pets
Restricted smoking
Mastercard & Visa

Enjoy century old country home. 35 acres of woods, fields and gardens, with natural country beauty offering pleasant relaxation. Enjoy deer, wild birds, turkey, blue heron and an occasional howl of a coyote, all from the porch swing on the upstairs verandah, or capture quiet moments and reading in your room. A home away from home!

# MR. TOAD'S SPINACH CASSEROLE

**3 pkgs. frozen spinach, chopped**
**1 small pkg. cream cheese, softened**
**8 oz. sour cream**
**1 can cream of mushroom soup**
**Parmesan cheese**
**Paprika to taste**

Thaw spinach and squeeze very dry. Mix with softened cream cheese; spread in flat serving dish. Mix sour cream and mushroom soup, spread on top of spinach. Sprinkle liberally with Parmesan cheese and paprika. Bake at 350° for 40 - 45 minutes. Good with scrambled eggs. Makes 8 servings. This is our most requested recipe!

---

Submitted by:

Toad Hall
301 N. Scoville Ave.
Oak Park, IL 60302
(708) 386-8623
Cynthia V. Mungerson
$55.00 to $65.00

Full breakfast
3 rooms, 3 private baths
No children
No pets
No smoking

1909 gracious Colonial offers old-world atmosphere and services. Victorian antiques, Oriental rugs, Laura Ashley furnishings. Candlelight breakfast served "en suite" or in oak-paneled dining room. Bridal suite. Near shops and restaurants. Winner of Amoco "Favorite B&B" award.

# SEAFOOD SOUFFLÉ

**5 slices bread, cubed, without crusts**
**1/2 lb. small shrimp**
**1/2 lb. - 1 lb. imitation crab meat, chunked**
**1/4 lb. shredded Swiss cheese**
**1/4 lb. shredded Cheddar cheese**
**4 beaten eggs**
**1/4 teaspoon dry mustard**
**2 cups milk**
**1/2 teaspoon salt**

In an 8" x 11" oblong buttered pan, layer bread cubes, seafood and cheeses, in that order. Mix together eggs, dry mustard, milk, and salt. Pour over mixture in pan and bake at 325° - 350° for 1 1/4 - 1 1/2 hours. You may make this ahead of time and refrigerate, however; allow extra baking time. Makes 8 - 12 servings.

---

Submitted by:

Sugar Maple Inn
607 Maple
Lena, IL 61048
(815) 369-2786
Richard & Debra Leverton
$30.00 to $50.00

Full breakfast
3 rooms, 1 private bath
Children allowed
No pets
No smoking

Queen Anne style, 3-story home built by a wealthy egg merchant around 1880, where the first known central vacuum cleaner was invented, but not patented. Verandah porch perfect for reading & relaxing. Near golf, tennis, swimming & Lake Le-Aqua-Na State Park.

# ASSORTED BAKED GOODS

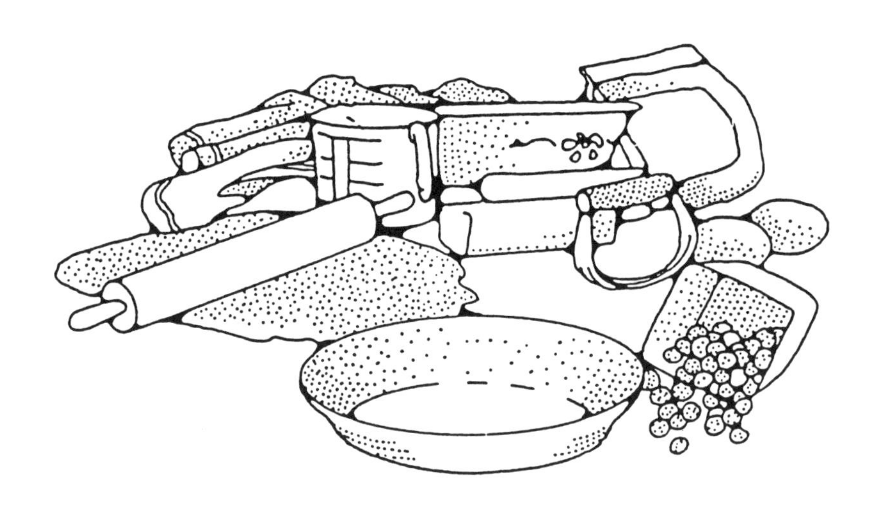

# BANANA BREAD

**1 egg**
**1 cup sugar**
**1/4 cup melted butter**
**1 teaspoon vanilla**
**3 bananas, mashed**
**1 1/2 cups flour**
**1 teaspoon baking soda**
**1 teaspoon salt**
**1/2 cup chopped pecans or walnuts**

Beat egg slightly. Add sugar, melted butter, and vanilla. Blend bananas and add to egg mixture. Sift together flour, soda, and salt and add to mixture. Add nuts. Bake at 375° in greased loaf pan (4 1/2" x 9" x 5") for 45 minutes or until inserted wooden toothpick comes out clean. Cool and remove from pan. Slice bread when cooled at desired thickness. Makes 6 - 8 servings.

---

Submitted by:

Living Legacy Homestead
R.R. 2, Box 146A
Mt. Carmel, IL 62863
(618) 298-2476
Edna Schmidt Anderson
$35.00 to $65.00

Full breakfast
3 rooms, 2 private baths
Children allowed
No pets
No smoking

Country living in turn-of-the-century restored German homestead, originally a log home from 1870's! Antique & period furniture, interior walls and loft of log house are exposed. Gift shop, spacious yard, flower, vegetable & herb gardens. Orchard, meadow, barnyard, and wildlife. Several original farm buildings on 10 acre site.

# BASIL OAT SCONES

**1/2 cup + 2 tablespoons oatmeal (divided)**
**2 cups flour**
**2 1/2 teaspoons baking powder**
**1 tablespoon sugar**
**1/2 teaspoon salt**
**1 tablespoon dried basil**
**1 tablespoon dried parsley**
**1/4 cup softened butter**
**1/2 cup cream**
**1 egg, slightly beaten**
**Water**

Preheat oven to 450°. Combine 1/2 cup oats, remainder of dry ingredients, and herbs in bowl. Stir well with fork. Add butter in pieces to dry mixture and cut in with pastry blender or use fingertips until mixture looks like crumbs. Stir in cream and egg. Mix until moistened. Gather dough into a ball and press until it stays together. Turn dough out onto floured board. Knead lightly about 15 seconds, 8 - 10 times. Pat dough into circle 8" across. Brush with water and sprinkle with 2 tablespoons oats. Cut into 8 wedges. Place scones about 1" apart on ungreased baking sheet. Bake 10 - 12 minutes or until tops are lightly browned. Wonderful served with apricot jam!

---

Submitted by:

Sweet Basil Hill Farm B&B Inn
15937 W. Washington St.
Gurnee, IL 60031
(708) 244-3333
Bob & Teri Jones
$65.00 to $105.00

Continental plus breakfast
3 suites, 3 private baths
Children allowed
No pets
No smoking
Mastercard & Visa

Country getaway atop a hill on 7 acres, has sheep, llamas, & gardens. Common Room, decorated with English Pine antiques, beckons with cozy fireplace. Featured in Country Home & Innsider Magazines, the Chicago Tribune & Sun-Times. ABBA rated with 3 crowns. Our first concern is your comfort & privacy!

# BUNDLING BOARD INN BREAKFAST SHORTCAKE

**Shortcake:**
**4 cups Bisquick**
**1/2 cup quick oatmeal**
**1 tablespoon wheat germ**
**1 cup milk**
**1/4 cup sugar**
**6 tablespoons melted butter**

**Fruit Syrup topping:**
**2 cups chopped strawberries, blueberries, raspberries, or use a mixture**
**2 cups water**
**1 cup sugar**
**2 teaspoons cornstarch**

Combine shortcake ingredients, and spoon generously into 2 greased muffin pans. Bake at 425° for 15 minutes. Prepare fruit and add water, sugar and cornstarch. Cook in microwave oven on High for 5 minutes, or on stovetop, until clear and juicy. Open shortcake biscuits, and ladle fruit syrup topping on top. Add coconut, chopped nuts, or your choice of other toppings, and garnish with a dollop of yogurt. Makes 20 - 24 servings.

---

Submitted by:

The Bundling Board Inn
220 E. South St.
Woodstock, IL 60098
(815) 338-7054
Karen Knight
$45.00 to $55.00

Continental breakfast
6 rooms, 3 private baths
Children allowed
No pets
No smoking
Mastercard, Visa, Discover

Restored 1910 Queen Anne, furnished with lovely Victorian antiques. 3 blocks to historic Woodstock town square, and Opera House. Great countryside for hiking and biking. Northern Illinois' best-kept secret!

# CHOCOLATE ZUCCHINI BREAD

**3 eggs**
**2 cups sugar**
**1 cup oil**
**2 cups zucchini, not peeled, and put through food processor**
**2 squares baking chocolate, melted**
**3 cups flour**
**1 teaspoon salt**
**1 teaspoon soda**
**1/4 teaspoon baking powder**
**1 teaspoon vanilla**
**1 cup coarsely chopped nuts**

Beat eggs until foamy. Add sugar, oil, zucchini, and melted chocolate. Mix. Add flour, salt, soda, baking powder, vanilla, and nuts. Bake in loaf pan at 350° for one hour.

---

Submitted by:

The Potter House
1906 7th Avenue
Rock Island, IL
61201
(309) 788-1906 or
(800) 747-0339
Gary & Nancy Pheiffer
$55.00 to $100.00

Full breakfast
5 rooms, 5 private baths, plus Guest House
Children allowed
No pets
No smoking
Mastercard, Visa, Am Ex, Discover

Restored 1907 Colonial Revival listed on National Register of Historic Places. Quality features such as stained glass, leather wallcoverings, six fireplaces, and mahogany paneled dining room. Rooms have phones and cable TV. Located near riverboat casino, dinner theatre, and fine dining.

# CINNAMON BRUNCH COFFEE CAKE

**Cake:**
**1 pkg. yellow cake mix**
**1 pkg. instant vanilla pudding**
**3/4 cup oil**
**3/4 cup orange juice**
**4 eggs**
**1 tablespoon butter flavoring**

**Filling:**
**1/4 cup sugar**
**2 teaspoons cinnamon**
**1/2 cup chopped nuts**

**Glaze:**
**1 cup powdered sugar**
**2 teaspoons milk**
**Vanilla to taste**

Mix cake ingredients together and beat eight minutes on medium speed of mixer. Thoroughly oil bundt pan. (Do not flour pan.) Pour half of batter in pan and layer half of filling mixture on top. Pour remaining batter into pan and top with remaining half of filling. Bake at 350° for 45 minutes. Cool on wire rack. Mix glaze ingredients. Glaze after cooled cake is removed from pan. This cake freezes well. Makes 16 servings.

---

Submitted by:

Standish House B&B
540 West Carroll St.
Lanark, IL
61046
(800) 468-2307
Eve Engles
$55.00 to $65.00

Full breakfast
5 rooms, 1 private bath
Well-behaved children allowed
No pets
No smoking
Mastercard & Visa

1882 Victorian home, furnished with 18th century antiques and queen canopy beds. Myles Standish heritage carried throughout. On Route 52, 120 miles west of Chicago. Relaxing small town atmosphere. Walking distance to business district and restaurants. Honeymoon/anniversary/theatre/golf packages available.

# CRANBERRY BREAKFAST PIE

**2 cups fresh cranberries**
**1/2 cup chopped walnuts**
**1/2 cup brown sugar**
**1 stick melted butter or margarine**
**1 cup white sugar**
**1 teaspoon almond extract**
**1 cup flour**
**2 beaten eggs**

Grease large pie pan or 9" x 9" cake pan. Put washed cranberries in pan and sprinkle with walnuts and brown sugar. Combine butter, white sugar, almond extract, flour, and eggs, and pour over contents in pan. Bake at 350° for 45 minutes. Can be served with vanilla yogurt as a topping. Makes 8 servings.

---

Submitted by:

Grandma Joan's Homestay
2204 Brett Dr.
Champaign, IL 61821
(217) 356-5828
Joan Erickson
$45.00 to $50.00

Full breakfast
3 rooms, 1 private bath
Children, over 10
No pets
Restricted smoking

Quiet, comfortable, contemporary 10 room home has artwork & furnishing reflecting cultural heritage, travels, & talent of proprietor. Relax with 2 fireplaces, several decks, screened-in porch, and hot tub. Beverage upon arrival and cookies & milk at bedtime. Healthy breakfast in French country kitchen, on porch, or in dining room.

# FRUIT PUDDING

**1 cup canned fruit (cherries, apricots, pineapple, etc.)**
**2 cups liquid (fruit juice or water)**
**1 cup sugar**
**4 tablespoons butter**
**1/4 cup shortening**
**1 cup sugar**
**2 cups flour**
**2 teaspoons baking powder**
**1/2 teaspoon salt**
**1 cup milk**

Combine fruit, liquid, 1 cup sugar and 4 tablespoons butter. Cook 10 minutes. Cream 1/4 cup shortening and 1 cup sugar. Add flour, baking powder and salt, alternately with milk. Pour into greased 9" x 9" pan. Pour cooked fruit and syrup over the top. Bake for 30 minutes at 375°. Makes 9 servings.

---

Submitted by:

Mill Creek Inn
504 N. Mill
Nashville, IL 62263
(618) 327-8424 or
(618) 327-8718
Bill & Barbara Garlich
$52.00 to $55.00

Full breakfast
2 rooms, 2 private baths
Children allowed
Pets allowed, with boarding available
Smoking allowed
Mastercard & Visa

Buit in 1856, with brass door hardware from Germany, a butler's pantry, four fireplaces, and cast iron balcony. Picturesque view of mill pond and surrounding woods can be enjoyed from the spacious backyard. Apple shed-smokehouse and gazebo located on the grounds. Guest rooms have color TV and antique furnishings.

# LEMON-SPICE COFFEE CAKE

**Batter:**
**2 cups flour**
**1 cup brown sugar**
**1 1/2 teaspoons lemon peel**
**3/4 teaspoon allspice**
**1/2 teaspoon baking soda**
**1/4 teaspoon salt**
**8 oz. lemon yogurt**
**1/2 cup oleo or butter, softened**
**1 egg**

**Crumb topping:**
**1/2 cup chopped pecans**
**1/3 cup brown sugar**
**1/4 cup flour**
**3 tablespoons oleo**

In large mixing bowl combine flour, brown sugar, lemon peel, allspice, baking soda, and salt. Mix, then add yogurt, oleo and egg. Beat until mixed. Pour batter into greased 9" x 12" pan. Mix topping ingredients in a small bowl until crumbly. Sprinkle over batter. Bake in 350° oven for 35 - 40 minutes. Makes 24 squares.

---

Submitted by:

Hellman Guest House
318 Hill Street
Galena, IL 61036
(815) 777-3638
Merilyn Tommaro/
Rachel Stilson
$75.00 to $95.00

Continental plus breakfast
4 rooms, 4 private baths
Children, over 12
No pets
Restricted smoking
Mastercard, Visa, Am Ex

Restored 1895 Queen Anne, Galena brick home, reflecting the beauty and elegance of the 19th century. Inviting rooms with antiques, original woodwork and stained-beveled glass windows, restored front porch; all just 2 1/2 blocks from downtown Galena.

# LEMON YOGURT BREAD

- **3 cups all-purpose flour**
- **1 teaspoon salt**
- **1 teaspoon baking soda**
- **1/2 teaspoon baking powder**
- **1 cup sesame or poppy seeds**
- **3 eggs**
- **1 cup oil**
- **1 cup sugar**
- **2 cups lemon yogurt**
- **2 tablespoons freshly squeezed lemon juice**

Sift together flour, salt, soda, and baking powder. Stir in seeds. Beat eggs in large bowl. Add oil and sugar; cream well. Add yogurt and lemon juice. Spoon into 2 greased loaf pans or 1 large bundt pan. Bake in 325° oven for one hour. Makes 2 loaves.

---

Submitted by:

Captain Gear Guest House
1000 S. Bench St.
Galena, IL 61036
(815) 777-0222
Alyce Green
$64.00 to $99.00

Continental plus breakfast
3 rooms, 3 private baths
No children
No pets
Restricted smoking
Mastercard & Visa

One of Galena's outstanding mansions, built in 1855. Situated on 4 secluded acres, but only 3/4 mile from downtown shops. One private bath has double whirlpool.

# NORWEGIAN COFFEE CAKE

**2 1/2 cups flour**
**1 teaspoon salt**
**1 tablespoon cinnamon**
**3/4 cup white sugar**
**1 cup brown sugar**
**2/3 cup cooking oil**
**1 teaspoon baking soda**
**1 teaspoon baking powder**
**1 egg**
**1 cup buttermilk**
**1/2 cup chopped nuts**

Sift together flour, salt, cinnamon and white sugar. Add brown sugar and oil, mixing until mixture is of crumb consistency. Reserve 3/4 cup of mixture for topping. Add to remaining flour mixture the baking soda, baking powder, egg and buttermilk, mixing thoroughly. Pour batter into a well-greased 9" x 12" pan. Sprinkle with reserved topping and chopped nuts. Bake 30 minutes at 350°. Enjoy warm or cold. Makes 12 - 18 servings.

---

Submitted by:

The Olde Brick House
502 N. High
Port Byron, IL 61275
(309) 523-3236
Fred & LaVerne Waldbusser
$40.00 to $50.00

Continental breakfast
3 rooms, 2 shared baths
Children allowed
No pets
Restricted smoking
Mastercard & Visa

Historic home, circa 1855, on 1.5 shaded acres just off I-80 on the Mississippi River. Close to antiquing, the Quad Cities, and the riverboats. Enjoy eagle watching. Classic charm of old-fashioned porches & sitting rooms, cozy "attic" bedroom, and the sunny delight of the master bedroom, we invite you for pure rest and relaxation.

# OAT SCONES

**2/3 cup butter or margarine, melted**
**1/3 cup milk**
**1 egg**
**1 1/2 cups all-purpose flour**
**1 1/4 cups quick Quaker oats, uncooked**
**1/3 cup sugar**
**1 tablespoon baking powder**
**1 teaspoon cream of tartar**
**1/2 teaspoon salt**
**1/2 cup raisins or currants**

Combine dry ingredients. Add butter, milk and egg to dry ingredients. Mix until just moist. Stir in raisins. Shape dough to form ball, pat out on lightly floured surface to form 8" circle. Cut into 8 to 12 wedges; bake on greased cookie sheet in preheated 425° oven 12 - 15 minutes, or until golden brown. Serve warm with butter, preserves or honey.

---

Submitted by:

The Golds Bed & Breakfast
R.R. 3, Box 69
Champaign, IL 61821
(217) 586-4345
Rita & Bob Gold
$40.00 to $45.00

Continental breakfast
3 rooms, 1 private bath
Children, over 4
No pets
Restricted smoking

Carefully restored 9-room, 1874 farm house offers quiet, private country location just off I-74. After a night of sound sleep in a four-poster bed, enjoy breakfast on an 1820 harvest table, and share experiences with other guests and the hosts. Light and airy rooms, antique country furniture.

# PEANUT BUTTER BREAD

**2 cups flour**
**4 teaspoons baking powder**
**1 teaspoon salt**
**1/3 cup sugar**
**1/2 cup peanut butter (chunky works best)**
**1 1/2 cups milk**

Mix and sift dry ingredients. Add peanut butter and cut in well with pastry blender. Add milk and beat thoroughly. Pour into greased loaf cake pan and bake at 350° for about 1 hour. This makes good toast. Makes 1 loaf.

---

Submitted by:

Friddle Creek Lodge B&B
P.O. Box 110, IL Hwy. 100
Browning, IL 62624
(217) 323-4232
J. Kelly & Mary J. Stambaugh
$50.00 to $60.00

Full breakfast
3 rooms, 3 private baths
Children, over 12
No pets
No smoking
Mastercard & Visa

Located on a 320 acre grain and cattle farm. Wildlife such as woodducks, mallards, quail, deer, etc., are frequent visitors to our acreage. There are ponds, creeks, and country lanes, as well as views of the Illinois River Valley to offer our visitors.

# PINEAPPLE CARROT BREAD

**3 eggs**
**2 cups sugar**
**1 cup oil**
**1 cup grated carrots**
**1 cup crushed pine-apple, undrained**
**1 cup chopped pecans**
**2 teaspoons vanilla**
**1 1/2 teaspoons cinnamon**
**1 1/2 teaspoons baking soda**
**1 1/2 teaspoons salt**
**3 cups flour**

Mix all ingredients together. Grease and flour 3 bread pans. Bake at 350° for one hour. This can be made into 24 muffins as well. Bake at 350° for 15 minutes. They also freeze well.

---

Submitted by:

The Farm B&B
Route 1, Box 112
Mt. Carroll, IL 61053
(815) 244-9885
Herb & Betty Weinand
$75.00 to $95.00

Full breakfast
2 rooms, 2 private baths
No children
No pets
Smoking allowed
Mastercard & Visa

Country elegance with 2 charming & unique accommodations: The Cottage and The Barn Spa Suite. Both with cozy fireplace, magnificent view, sitting & dining areas, patio, and complete privacy. 2-person jacuzzi spa adjoins The Barn Spa Suite. Outdoor hot tub.

# QUICK STICKY PECAN ROLLS

**1/2 cup melted butter or margarine**
**1/2 cup brown sugar**
**1 tablespoon water**
**1/2 cup chopped pecans**
**10 small canned biscuits**

Place butter in saucepan on medium heat until melted. Add brown sugar and mix well. Cook for 2 minutes, then add water. When mixture bubbles, add chopped pecans. Have muffin tins buttered, and cut biscuits into fourths. Place cooked mixture in bottom of each muffin cup. Roll dough into balls. Place 4 balls of dough in each tin opening. Spoon cooked mixture on top, covering dough. Bake at 350° until medium brown. Remove from tin. Spoon extra pecan mixture back onto rolls. Can be frozen or reheated. Makes 10 rolls.

---

Submitted by:

Historic Home Park Place
R.R. 1, Box 140
Towanda, IL 61776
(309) 728-2844
Doris Phelps
$45.00 to $65.00

Full breakfast
5 rooms, 4 private baths
Children allowed
Pets allowed, if restricted
Smoking, restricted areas only

Brick Victorian includes marble fireplaces and 14' ceilings in parlors, library & formal dining room. Winding walnut stairway, recreation room in basement, TV and VCR. Grill out during summer months, picnic, stroll through the grounds, or just relax. Varied recreation nearby.

# FRUITS & BEVERAGES

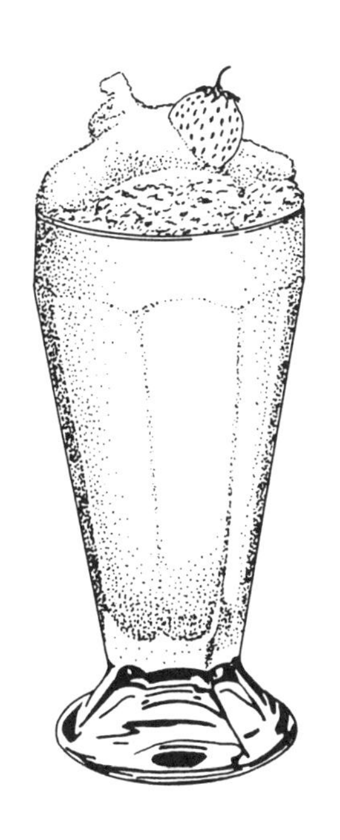

# BREAKFAST PARFAIT

**1/2 cup favorite granola**
**1/4 cup plain nonfat yogurt**
**1/2 cup sliced strawberries**
**1/2 cup ripe banana, sliced**

Place half of granola in parfait glass. Top with half of yogurt. Arrange half of strawberries and the banana over yogurt. Top with remaining granola, yogurt and strawberries. Garnish with fresh mint or whole large strawberry. Makes 1 serving.

---

Submitted by:

Victorian Inn B&B
702 - 20 Street
Rock Island, IL 61201
(309) 788-7068
David & Barbara Parker
$45.00 to $65.00

Full breakfast
5 rooms, 5 private baths
Children allowed
No pets
Restricted smoking
Mastercard & Visa

Stained glass tower invites travelers inside; guest and common rooms are filled with original antiques. Breakfast served in spacious dining room on Haviland china and fine silver. Peruse the dollhouse filled with unique miniatures. A relaxing getaway, taking one back to a bygone golden era. Welcome. . .

# COLD SPICED PEARS

**1 lb., 13 oz. can pear halves, drained**
**1/2 cup sugar**
**1/4 cup vinegar**
**1 teaspoon whole cloves**
**1 teaspoon whole allspice**
**2" piece of cinnamon**

Drain pears, and reserve syrup. Set pears aside. Measure 1 cup pear syrup into large saucepan. Add sugar, vinegar, cloves, allspice, and cinnamon. Bring to a boil. Reduce heat, simmer 10 minutes. Add pears, cook 3 - 5 minutes or until pears are heated thoroughly. Remove from heat. Cool. Refrigerate several hours before serving. Serve with all meat dishes. Makes 8 servings.

---

Submitted by:

Bed & Breakfast at Edie's
233 E. Harpole
Williamsville, IL 62693
(217) 566-2538
Edie Senalik
$40.00 to $55.00

Continental plus breakfast
4 rooms
Children allowed
No pets
No smoking

An 80 year old Mission style homestead located in a peaceful, safe community with American small-town flavor. Large, comfortable, and homey bedrooms feature queen-size beds, percale sheets and down pillows. After a bountiful breakfast, enjoy a second cup of freshly brewed coffee on the large veranda or the rear patio.

# E-Z PINEAPPLE FRUIT SALADS

**Whole pineapples, cut into halves**
**Various fruit of choice:**
**Sliced peaches**
**Strawberries**
**Apples**
**Banana**
**Raspberries**
**Blueberries**
**Kiwi**
**Grapes**
**Pineapple**
**Oranges**
**Blackberries**

Cut pineapples into halves, remove insides, and set shells aside. Refill with sliced or diced fruit of your choice. These are lovely, colorful, and healthful. Use as many pineapples as needed to make the number of servings you want.

---

Submitted by:

Shurts House B&B
710 W. Oregon Street
Urbana, IL 61801
(217) 328-5139 or
(217) 367-8793
Bruce & Denni Shurts
Suite: M-Th-$100.00/night
Fri-Sat-Sun-$150.00/night
Room: M-Th-$75.00/night
Fri-Sat-Sun-$100.00/night

Continental plus breakfast
5 rooms, 2 private baths
Children allowed,
Sitting service available
No pets
Restricted smoking
Mastercard, Visa, Am Ex

English Tudor Style inn built in 1901. Exterior pool, bicycles built for two, and free tours of our city, in a "Model A" coupe. Furnished with some rare antiques, a large and comfortable home. We pride ourselves on being a friendly, cozy inn.

# FRESH FRUIT CUP

**2 bananas, peeled, sliced**
**1 orange, peeled, diced**
**2 red apples, diced**
**1 kiwi fruit, peeled, diced**

Combine all ingredients. Fold together gently. Serve with French toast and Canadian bacon. Makes 4 servings.

---

Submitted by:

Ruth's Bed 'n Breakfast
1506 W. Alta Rd.
Peoria, IL 61615
(309) 243-5977
Ruth & William Giles
$25.00 to $30.00

Continental plus breakfast
3 rooms, shared baths
Children allowed
Pets allowed
Restricted smoking

Private home on acreage. Air-conditioned. Queen or double beds. 20 minutes or less from city and river attractions. Homey atmosphere. Children welcome.

# HOT CHOCOLATE MIX

**8 qt. box powdered milk mix**
**6 oz. jar coffee creamer**
**1 lb. Nestle's Quick hot chocolate mix**
**6 - 8 oz. instant chocolate pudding mix**

Mix ingredients together and store in container. Use 1/3 cup hot chocolate mix for each cup of hot water. Keeps up to four months in tightly sealed container.

---

Submitted by:

Ridgeview Bed & Breakfast
8833 S. Massbach Rd.
Elizabeth, IL
61028
(815) 598-3150
Betty Valy
$60.00 to $89.00

Continental plus breakfast
4 rooms, 4 private baths
Children and pets allowed by special arrangement
Restricted smoking
Mastercard, Visa, Am Ex, Discover

Off-the-beaten-path country B&B, unique spacious rooms. Loft Suite has a 10-mile view. Shopping, antiques, golfing, horseback riding, Mississippi River, parks, fine dining and more, all within 30 minute drive in scenic Galena/Jo Daviess County. Located on well-groomed, hard-surface road; great for bicycling.

# STRAWBERRY LEMONADE

**4 cups strawberries, stemmed and rinsed**
**1 cup cold water**
**6 oz. can lemonade concentrate, undiluted & chilled**
**2 cups club soda, chilled**

Place all ingredients except club soda in blender. Blend well. Fill a clear glass pitcher with the strawberry mixture and chill. When ready to serve, pour the club soda into the pitcher, stir once, and pour into glasses of cracked ice. Makes 2 quarts. Make plenty, there's always a call for refills!

Submitted by:

Old Church House Inn B&B
1416 East Mossville Road
Mossville, IL 61552
(309) 579-2300
Dean & Holly Ramseyer
$49.00 to $89.00

Gourmet continental breakfast
2 rooms, 1 private bath
No pets
No smoking
Mastercard & Visa

Nestled in the scenic Illinois River Valley 5 miles north of Peoria, this 1869 historic church welcomes you to the plush warmth of a Victorian era. Enjoy colorful flower gardens, afternoon tea, queen featherbeds, and pampering amenities in Peoria's finest B&B. Bicycling on Rock Island Bike Trail is 5 minutes away, or indulge in shopping, dining, and Peoria's riverboat cruises!

# WINTER MORNING PEACHES

**2 - 16 oz. cans sliced peaches**
**2 tablespoons margarine or butter**
**1/3 cup brown sugar**
**1/2 teaspoon cinnamon**
**2 tablespoons cornstarch**
**1/4 cup cold water**

In saucepan over medium heat, heat peaches, margarine, brown sugar, and cinnamon. Stir cornstarch into cold water and add to peaches. Cook and stir until thickened. Cool slightly and spoon into individual dishes. Serve warm. Makes 6 - 8 servings.

---

Submitted by:

Welcome Inn
506 W. Main
Oblong, IL 62449
(618) 592-3301
Laird & Donna Dart
$48.00 to $58.00

Full breakfast
5 rooms, 5 private baths
Children allowed
No pets
No smoking
Mastercard & Visa

Large 2-story brick home constructed in 1913, renovated with comfort and safety in mind. Tastefully decorated inside with a Victorian flair, inn is surrounded by a unique stone wall. Relax on verandah, in gazebo, or visit in parlor. Enjoy the peace and quiet of small town "country livin'."

# NOT JUST FOR BREAKFAST...

# APPLES AND POTATOES

**4 medium potatoes (about 4 cups, cut in 1" cubes)**
**2 tart apples, sliced**
**1 tablespoon sugar**
**1 cup water**
**1 teaspoon salt**
**4 slices bacon, cut into 1" pieces**
**1 medium onion, sliced**
**1 tablespoon margarine or butter, softened**
**Nutmeg to taste**

Heat 1 inch salted water (1 teaspoon salt to 1 cup water) to boiling. Add potatoes, apples and sugar. Heat to boiling; reduce heat. Cover and cook until potatoes are tender, 10 - 15 minutes; drain. Fry bacon until crisp; drain. Sauté onion in bacon fat until tender. Place potatoes and apples in serving bowl. Dot with margarine, sprinkle with nutmeg. Top with bacon and onion. Serves 4 - 6 persons.

---

Submitted by:

Alice's Place
1915 Winchester
Champaign, IL 61821
(217) 359-3332
Alice Gaines
$45.00 to $55.00

Continental plus breakfast
3 rooms, 1 private bath
No pets
Restricted smoking

A friendly atmosphere in a comfortable setting. Abundant flower gardens and plant-filled sun porch lend a feeling of home and country in an urban environment. Convenient to University of Illinois, Interstates 57, 72 and 74, as well as the heart of downtown.

# CHICKEN SOUP AND DUMPLINGS

- 2 cups chopped, cooked chicken
- 4 cups broth
- 1/2 cup diced celery
- 1/2 cup chopped carrots
- 1 medium chopped onion
- 1 large chopped raw potato
- Salt & pepper to taste

**Dumplings:**

- 1 egg, beaten
- 1 tablespoon margarine
- 4 tablespoons Cream of Wheat

Cook chicken, debone, and chop meat. Add vegetables with chicken to broth, and cook until tender. Mix egg, margarine, and Cream of Wheat. Drop dumplings by small pinches into soup. Cook 10 minutes more. Add salt & pepper to taste. And it's ready to serve! This is also good reheated. Makes 6 servings.

---

Submitted by:

Thelma's Bed & Breakfast
201 S. Broadway
West Salem, IL 62476
(618) 456-8401
Thelma Lodwig
$15.00 per person

Full breakfast
4 rooms, shared bath
Children allowed
No pets
No smoking

Two-story, 12 room brick, Prairie-style home. Large front porch and living areas available to guests. Meals are served by request.

# COPPER CARROTS

**2 lbs. carrots**
**1 green bell pepper**
**2 onions, sliced**

**Sauce:**
**1 can tomato soup**
**1/2 cup oil**
**3/4 cup cider vinegar**
**Salt & pepper to taste**
**2 teaspoons Worcestershire sauce**
**1 teaspoon prepared mustard**

Slice and cook carrots. Slice onion and pepper. Layer carrots, onion, and pepper. To serve cold: Pour sauce over top of vegetables and refrigerate. To serve hot: Combine sauce ingredients and heat to boiling point. Pour over vegetables. Delicious hot or cold. Makes 6 - 8 servings.

---

Submitted by:

The Thomas House
R.R. #1
Junction, IL 62954
(618) 272-7046
Jane Thomas
$40.00 to $55.00

Full breakfast
3 rooms, 1 private bath
Children allowed
No pets
Restricted smoking
Mastercard & Visa

Each attractive guest room is decorated in a different decor. The remainder of the hostess' home, available to guests, offers the best view of the Shawnee Hills, screened-in porch, gazebo/sun deck, wood fireplace, pool table, and satellite TV - southern Illinois hospitality at its finest!

# CREAM CHEESE PASTRY

**2 cups all-purpose flour**
**1/2 teaspoon salt**
**1/2 cup shortening**
**2 - 3 oz. pkgs. cream cheese**
**5 - 6 tablespoons cold water**

Combine flour and salt. Cut in shortening and cream cheese with pastry blender until mixture resembles coarse meal. Sprinkle cold water, one tablespoon at a time, evenly over surface. Stir with a fork until dry ingredients are moistened. Shape into a ball, chill. Yield: Pastry for one double crust pie.

---

Submitted by:

The Favorite Brother Inn
106 East Columbia
Arthur, IL 61911
(217) 543-2938
Rick & Vickie Weger
$40.00 to $45.00

Full breakfast
2 rooms, 1 private bath
Well-behaved children allowed
No pets
Restricted smoking

In the heart of Illinois Amish country, this inn offers warm hospitality and a generous view of passing horses & buggies. Bedrooms cheerfully decorated. Awaken to aroma of freshly ground coffee and homemade cream cheese & cinnamon rolls. Breakfasts are special!

# HERB AND DILL VEGETABLE AND CRACKER DIP

- **1 large container French onion dip**
- **8 oz. cream cheese**
- **1/2 cup mayonnaise**
- **2 teaspoons basil**
- **3 tablespoons dill weed**
- **1/2 teaspoon garlic powder**
- **2 tablespoons minced onion**

Mix ingredients well, and chill well.

---

Submitted by:

Enchanted Crest
RR #1, Box 216
Belle Rive, IL 62810
(618) 736-2647
W. Loyd & Carollyn Blackwell
$45.00

Full/Continental plus breakfast
2 rooms, shared bath
Children, over 4
No pets
Restricted smoking

Century old Victorian mansion with a 6 acre lawn, and 20+ different gardens with over 400 varieties of herbs, perennials & everlastings! 50+ year old barn conjures up visions of a Saturday night barn dance, 2 acre lake is surrounded by whispering pines. 50+ handmade quilts on display. On National List of Historical Places. Lunches and gourmet dinner by reservation only. Country Victorian teas & tours.

# HERB-CHEESE CHICKEN

**16 oz. cream cheese, room temperature**
**1/4 cup butter, room temperature**
**1 1/2 tablespoons whipping cream**
**1/4 teaspoon garlic powder**
**1/4 teaspoon oregano**
**1/4 teaspoon thyme**
**1/4 teaspoon marjoram**
**1/4 teaspoon dillweed**
**1/4 teaspoon basil**
**1/4 teaspoon pepper**
**8 - 4 oz. chicken breasts**
**Butter**
**Seasoned bread crumbs**
**Parsley for garnish**

Blend cream cheese, 1/4 cup butter, whipping cream, and spices until smooth. Flatten chicken breasts by placing between two sheets of waxed paper, and pounding with flat side of cleaver. Place 2 oz. of cheese filling at one edge of each breast. Roll up, folding in sides of breast to completely enclose filling. Brush with melted butter and press surface all over with bread crumbs. Bake 15 minutes at 350° until nicely browned. Garnish with fresh finely chopped parsley. Makes 8 servings.

---

Submitted by:

The Mansion of Golconda
515 Columbus
Golconda, IL
62938
(618) 683-4400
Don & Marilyn Kunz
$75.00

Full breakfast
3 rooms, 3 private baths
Children, over 12
No pets
Restricted smoking
Mastercard, Visa, Am Ex, Discover

The Mansion is one of the most historical buildings in Golconda, and its renovation in 1981 made it the ideal setting to establish a full-service restaurant and inn. The Romanesque structure with gabled slate roof dominates the riverside setting on the Ohio River. Romantic rooms draw guests from all over the country.

# HOLIDAY CHEESE BALL

**12 oz. cream cheese**
**6 oz. Bleu cheese, crumbled**
**6 oz. Cheddar cheese spread**
**2 tablespoons grated onion**
**1 teaspoon Accent**
**2 teaspoons Worcestershire sauce**
**1/4 cup parsley flakes**
**1/2 cup ground pecans**

Soften all three kinds of cheese at least 1 hour before mixing. Mix all above ingredients until thoroughly blended. Divide mixture in half rolling each half into a ball on waxed paper. Wrap in waxed paper, then wrap in a second layer of foil. Refrigerate at least 24 hours before serving. Remove from refrigerator 1 hour before serving, and roll in a mixture of 1/4 cup parsley and 1/2 cup pecans. Serve with various kinds of crackers.

---

Submitted by:

B&B MidWest Reservations
P.O. Box 95503
Hoffman Estates, IL
60195-0503
(800) 342-2632
Martha E. McDonald-Swan

Reservation service

Established in November, 1987, we are now serving the states of IL, IN, and OH. Customers may use the "one-stop-shopping" method, matching their needs to available homes in the area. Our knowledge of the homes' atmospheres and amenities results in unbiased descriptions. We free hosts to spend time with their grateful guests.

# HOT CHICKEN SALAD

- **4 cups cooked white meat chicken**
- **4 cups chopped celery**
- **1 cup toasted almonds**
- **1 teaspoon salt**
- **1 teaspoon Accent seasoning**
- **4 teaspoons grated onion**
- **2 cups Hellmann's mayonnaise**
- **1 cup grated American or Cheddar cheese**
- **1 1/2 cups crushed potato chips**

Mix all ingredients and pile high in Pyrex baking dish. Bake at 450° for 10 minutes or until heated through. This is good served with fruit. Makes 8 generous servings.

---

Submitted by:

Eagle's Nest
11125 N. Trigger Road
Dunlap, IL 61525
(309) 243-7376
John & Lou Ann Williams
$35.00 plus tax

Continental breakfast
2 rooms, 2 private baths
Children allowed
No pets
No smoking

Nestled in tranquil rural setting, with twin beds in each guest bedroom, and in-ground swimming pool, on 2 1/2 wooded acres. Hiking and cross country skiing available. Jubilee College and Wildlife Prairie Parks readily accessible. Breakfast served on screened porch, weather permitting.

# INDIVIDUAL HAM LOAVES

**1/3 lb. freshly ground pork**
**2/3 lb. freshly ground cooked ham**
**1/2 cup bread crumbs**
**1/2 cup milk**
**Pepper to taste**
**1/4 cup brown sugar**
**1/4 cup vinegar**
**1/4 teaspoon dry mustard**

Combine first five ingredients. Form one loaf, then divide it into 6 individual loaves. Place in Pyrex baking dish and bake at 350° for one hour. During the last few minutes of baking stir together brown sugar, vinegar and dry mustard, and pour over ham loaves. Baste with the sauce again just before serving. Makes 6 servings.

---

Submitted by:

Francie's Bed & Breakfast Inn
104 South Line Street
Du Quoin, IL 62832
(618) 542-6686
Tom & Francie Morgan
$50.00 to $80.00

Full breakfast
4 rooms, 4 private baths
Children allowed
No pets
Restricted smoking
Mastercard & Visa

Built as an orphanage in 1908, we are a large sturdy looking concrete block building with a big front porch and balcony, circular drive, in the middle of 3 acres. Walking distance to small town shopping and beautiful State Fairgrounds park. Dining room, craft shop, a/c, phones, friendly hosts.

# INGRID'S ANSJOVISROLL (SWEDISH ANCHOVY ROLL)

**Batter:**
**3 tablespoons butter**
**1/3 cup flour**
**1 cup milk**
**2/3 cup cream**
**2 tablespoons ansjovis juice**
**3 egg yolks**
**1/2 teaspoon baking powder**
**3 egg whites**

**Filling:**
**2 tablespoons butter**
**3 onions**
**1 tin ansjovis**
**2 oz. white or mild sharp cheese, grated**
**1/3 cup parsley**

Batter: Melt butter, add flour (roux). Add milk and cream for thick sauce. Let it boil 3 minutes, stir constantly. Add 2 tablespoons ansjovis juice. Add egg yolks, and baking powder. Let it cool. Whip egg whites and fold into cool mixture. Pat into 9" x 12" pan. Bake at 400° for 20 minutes. Watch closely. Turn upside down on a buttered parchment. Filling: Chop onions, sauté in butter until clear. Do not brown. Cut ansjovis into small pieces. Mix with onions. Pour over soft side of "cake". Sprinkle with chopped parsley and half of the cheese. Roll it up. Cover with balance of cheese and return to oven at 450° for 6 - 8 minutes. Cool a bit, cut and serve. Note: Anchovies are Swedish, and very subtle in flavor. They do not taste "fishy." Canned are available in Swede market - not Italian!

---

Submitted by:

Holden's Guest House
East Main Down Sun-Up Lane
Bishop Hill, IL 61419-0095
(309) 927-3500
Linda & Steve Holden
$50.00 to $180.00

Full breakfast
4 rooms, 1 private bath
Children allowed
No pets
Restricted smoking
Mastercard & Visa

Tranquil privacy combined with rural hospitality. Elegant breakfasts delivered on sterling trays. Restored 1869 farmstead on 1 1/2 acres adjacent to your hosts. Bishop Hill is a national historic landmark featuring 5 museums, 24 shops & fine luncheon places. Home available by the room, floor, or whole house - Illinois' best kept secret!

# LEMON-THYME POTATOES

**3 lbs. small red-skinned new potatoes, (not peeled), scrubbed**
**Salt & freshly ground pepper to taste**
**1 1/2 sticks butter**
**1/2 cup plus 1 tablespoon fresh lemon juice**
**1 1/2 teaspoons grated lemon zest**
**1 1/2 teaspoons crushed dried thyme**

Preheat oven to 375°. Quarter the potatoes and arrange them in a single layer in baking dish. Salt and pepper generously. Combine butter, lemon juice, and lemon zest in small saucepan and heat until butter has melted. Pour this mixture over the potatoes and sprinkle with thyme. Bake until potatoes are tender and lightly browned, 30 - 45 minutes. Remove from oven and serve hot. Serves 6 - 8.

---

Submitted by:

The Westerfield House, Inc.
8059 Jefferson Road
Freeburg, IL 62243
(618) 539-5643
Jim & Marilyn Westerfield
$150.00 to $170.00 (plus tax)
* Rates include 7-course dinner, overnight stay & breakfast

Full breakfast
3 rooms, 3 private baths
No children
No pets
Smoking allowed
Mastercard, Visa, Am Ex

Time is of the essence here. From our cupboards and candlelight, to the herbs drying from the ceiling, visit another place in time, a step backward in history to the period called the American Colonial era. Savor the historic setting & gourmet cuisine, & tour the herb garden.

# LENTIL SALAD

**1 cup lentils**
**2 cups water**
**2 beef bouillon cubes**
**2 cloves garlic, minced**
**1 medium onion, chopped**
**1 cup chopped tomato**
**1 cup chopped cucumber**
**2 tablespoons olive oil**
**1 1/2 teaspoons celery salt**
**1 cup cubed Cheddar cheese**

Rinse and drain lentils. Add lentils to next four ingredients in pan. Bring to a boil, cover and simmer 12 - 15 minutes. Drain if necessary, cool. Add next 5 ingredients. Cover and chill. Serve on pita bread or salad greens. Makes approximately 8 servings.

---

Submitted by:

Avery Guest House
606 S. Prospect
Galena, IL 61036
(815) 777-3883
Flo & Roger Jensen
$45.00 to $70.00

Continental plus breakfast
4 rooms, 2 baths
Children allowed
No pets
Restricted smoking

Pre-Civil War frame house provides homey atmosphere with good breakfast conversation, games and puzzles, and a porch swing overlooking Galena River Valley. TV in library, piano in large, high-ceilinged living room, is often the setting for sing-alongs. In Historic District, walk to historical sites, fine restaurants, shopping & antiques.

# POTATO WEDGES

**6 medium potatoes**
**Water**
**Dash of salt**
**3 tablespoons oil**
**1/2 teaspoon salt**
**Dash of black pepper**
**1/2 teaspoon dried oregano leaves**
**1/2 teaspoon dried thyme leaves**
**Dash of cayenne pepper**
**1/3 cup grated Parmesan cheese**
**2 tablespoons grated Cheddar cheese**

Scrub unpeeled potatoes and cut into even wedges. (If potato skins are too hard and old, peel the potatoes before cooking.) Boil wedges for 5 minutes in salted water. Drain. Pat dry. Spread wedges in a single layer on a lightly greased baking sheet. Sprinkle with oil, spices and herbs. Bake at 425° for about 15 minutes. Sprinkle with cheeses. Bake at 450° for 12 minutes or until potatoes are golden brown and cheeses are melted. Makes 4 servings.

---

Submitted by:

McNutt Guest House
409 W. Main St.
P.O. Box 466
Havana, IL 62644
(309) 543-3295 (daytime)
Karen Snedeker & Shirley Stephens
$35.00 to $125.00

Continental breakfast
3 rooms, 1 private bath, 1 shared bath
Children, over 12
No pets
Restricted smoking

Quiet relaxation in beautiful surroundings, with the banks of the scenic Illinois River just steps away. Within walking distance of antique and craft shops, and numerous restaurants featuring home-cooked fare. May reserve the entire Guest House which sleeps 8.

# SPAGHETTI SAUCE

**1 1/2 lbs. ground beef**
**2 medium onions, sliced thinly**
**2 cloves garlic**
**16 oz. can tomatoes**
**2 - 6 oz. cans tomato paste**
**2 beef bouillon cubes**
**3 cups water**
**1 teaspoon salt**
**1 teaspoon sugar**
**1 teaspoon oregano**
**1 teaspoon basil**
**1/4 teaspoon pepper**

Brown ground beef. Add onions and garlic, and cook until transparent. Add remaining ingredients. Bring to a boil. Turn down and simmer for 1 - 1 1/2 hours. Serve over spaghetti. Makes about 4 servings.

---

Submitted by:

Rockwell's Victorian
Bed & Breakfast
404 N. Washington
P.O. Box 392
Toulon, IL 61483
(309) 286-5201
Fred & Elizabeth Rockwell
$35.00 to $55.00

Full breakfast
3 rooms
Children, over 12
No pets
No smoking

Century old Victorian home, with original ambience, only the third owner. Near antique shops and Rock Island Bike Trail. 35 minutes to 2,000 acre Wildlife Prairie Park, and Peoria, with riverboat excursions, restaurants, & theaters. Homemade baked goods & local fresh fruit.

# SWISS FINGERS

**12 slices Baby Swiss cheese**
**Crab meat, to taste**
**Oregano, for garnish**

Lay out cheese slices. Put strips of crab meat in the center. Roll up and place on platter. Heat in microwave oven for one minute + or until cheese is soft. Garnish with fresh oregano leaves. Makes 6 servings.

---

Submitted by:

The Kaufmann House
1641 Hampshire
Quincy, IL 62301
(217) 223-2502
Emery & Bettie Kaufmann
$40.00

Continental plus breakfast
3 rooms, 1 private bath
Children allowed
No pets
Restricted smoking

Hospitality flows from this Historical District inn on beautiful tree-lined street. Experience quiet charm whether resting in one of the lovely bedrooms (2-Victorian style, 1-country), breakfasting in the ancestors' room or on the stone-terraced patio, or sitting by the fire. Piano, tandem bike, croquet. Antique shops and outstanding architectural homes close by.

# DESSERTS

# BUTTERSCOTCH DELIGHT

**1 angel food cake**
**12 oz. pkg. butterscotch morsels**
**1 large container Cool Whip**

Break angel food cake into small pieces. Put in shallow glass baking dish. Melt butterscotch morsels. Blend Cool Whip with melted butterscotch. Pour over angel food cake, making sure cake is well covered. Cool in refrigerator until set. Serve for dessert or with afternoon tea. This dessert is very rich and melts in your mouth. If you prefer, you may substitute chocolate morsels for butterscotch.

---

Submitted by:

Victorian Inn (Carlyle)
1111 Franklin
Carlyle, IL 62231
(618) 594-8506
Mary & Dennis Mincks
$55.00

Continental plus breakfast
2 rooms
Children, over 10
No pets
No smoking
Mastercard & Visa

Warm welcome awaits as you enter this century old Victorian home, a Clinton County historical landmark. 6 fireplaces, curving staircase and original stained glass windows are only the beginning! Delicate floral wallpaper sets the quiet tone of elegance in spacious guest rooms, beautifully furnished for authentic old-fashioned charm.

# CAN'T FAIL 5-MINUTE FUDGE

**2/3 cup undiluted evaporated milk**
**1 2/3 cups sugar**
**1/2 teaspoon salt**
**1 1/2 cups marshmallows (16 medium)**
**1 1/2 cups semi-sweet chocolate pieces**
**1 teaspoon vanilla**
**Garnishes: Chopped nuts, crushed peppermint candy or coconut**

Mix together evaporated milk, sugar, and salt in saucepan over medium heat. Bring to a boil. Cook 5 minutes stirring constantly. (Note: Begin timing when mixture starts bubbling around the edge of the pan). Remove from heat. Add marshmallows, chocolate pieces and vanilla. Stir vigorously one minute or until marshmallows melt. Pour into 8" square pan. Garnish with your choice of nuts, peppermint candy, or coconut.

---

Submitted by:

Johnson's Country Home
109 E. Main St.
Oakland, IL 61943
(217) 346-3274
Reece & June Johnson
$30.00 to $35.00 (extra person in room - $10.00)

Continental plus breakfast
2 rooms
Children allowed
No pets
Restricted smoking

2-story brick Italianate style home, circa 1874, with a varied 117-year history. During the Great Depression, it was a multi-family dwelling, a restaurant, UFW Post, and used for storage. Today it is a lovely home, listed on the Coles County Register of Historic Places.

# CARROT CAKE WITH CREAM CHEESE FROSTING

**1 1/2 cups vegetable oil**
**2 cups sugar**
**3 eggs**
**2 teaspoons vanilla**
**2 cups flour**
**2 teaspoons cinnamon**
**2 teaspoons baking soda**
**1 teaspoon salt**
**2 cups shredded carrots**
**20 oz. can crushed pineapple (drained)**
**1 cup chopped nuts**
**1 cup raisins**

**Cream Cheese Frosting:**
**1/4 cup butter**
**8 oz. cream cheese (softened)**
**3 cups powdered sugar**
**1 teaspoon vanilla**

In large bowl, thoroughly combine oil, sugar, eggs, and vanilla. Sift together flour, cinnamon, baking soda, and salt. Add to first mixture and mix well. Stir in shredded carrots, pineapple, nuts, and raisins. Pour into greased and floured 9" x 13" x 2" pan, or several smaller loaf pans. Bake at 350° for 50 - 60 minutes. until center of cake is firm to the touch. Cool in pan. Beat all frosting ingredients together until creamy. Frost cooled cake.

---

Submitted by:

Brierwreath Manor B&B
216 N. Bench St.
Galena, IL 61036
(815) 777-0608
Mike & Lyn Cook
$75.00 to $80.00

Full breakfast
3 rooms, 3 private baths
No children
No pets
No smoking

Only 1 short block from Galena's historic Main Street. Queen Anne style house (circa 1884), with wraparound porch. Early morning coffee served in upstairs hall before breakfast. Suites with queen size beds.

# CHIFFON CAKE

- **2 cups flour**
- **1 1/2 cups sugar**
- **1 tablespoon baking powder**
- **1 teaspoon salt**
- **3/4 cup cold water**
- **1/2 cup oil**
- **1 tablespoon vanilla**
- **2 teaspoons grated lemon peel**
- **8 egg yolks, beaten**
- **8 egg whites**
- **1/2 teaspoon cream of tartar**

Combine flour, sugar, baking powder and salt. Set aside. Combine water, oil, vanilla, lemon peel and egg yolks. Add to flour mixture. Whip egg whites and cream of tartar and fold into other ingredients. Bake in ungreased 10" tube pan for 60 minutes at 325°. Makes 12 servings.

---

Submitted by:

Bluffdale Vacation Farm
RR #1
Eldred, IL 62027
(217) 983-2854
Bill & Lindy Hobson
$60.00

Full breakfast
8 rooms, 8 private baths
Children allowed
No pets
Restricted smoking

Our farm for eight generations, 320 acres, with winding woodland trails for hiking or horseback, pond for fishing, wildflowers; a place of outdoor fun for the whole family. Pool, whirlpool in season, barn, haymow, farm animals. Bountiful country cooking, air-conditioning.

# CHOCOLATE-CINNAMON BARS

**2 cups sifted flour**
**1 teaspoon baking powder**
**1 1/3 cups sugar (divided)**
**4 teaspoons cinnamon (divided)**
**1/2 cup shortening**
**1/2 cup soft butter or margarine**
**1 egg**
**1 egg, separated**
**1 cup (6 oz.) chocolate chips or mini-morsels**
**1/2 cup chopped nuts**

Sift together flour, baking powder, 1 cup sugar, and 3 teaspoons cinnamon. Add shortening, butter, 1 egg and 1 egg yolk. Blend well. Turn into greased 9" x 13" pan and press out evenly. Beat egg white slightly, and brush over mixture in pan. Combine 1/3 cup sugar and 1 teaspoon cinnamon, chocolate chips and nuts. Sprinkle over egg white. Bake for 25 minutes at 350°. Cut into bars when cool. Makes 24 bars.

---

Submitted by:

Barb's Bed & Breakfast
606 S. Russell
Champaign, IL 61821
(217) 356-0376
Barb & Merle Eyestone
$45.00

Hearty continental breakfast
2 rooms
Children, over 12
No pets
No smoking

Cozy cottage in quiet, attractive West Champaign neighborhood. Guest rooms are a gentle blend of country and traditional featuring antiques, handmade quilts and family keepsakes. Near golf, swimming, bike & walking trails, parks, specialty shops, theatres, museums, and University of Illinois events and activities.

# COCONUT CREAM PIE

**2 - 9" pie crusts, baked**
**1 1/2 cups sugar**
**6 tablespoons corn-starch**
**1/2 teaspoon salt**
**4 cups milk**
**3 egg yolks**
**4 tablespoons butter or margarine**
**2 teaspoons vanilla**
**3 cups coconut**
**Whipped topping**

Combine dry ingredients in medium saucepan. Add milk, stirring constantly until it boils. Boil 2 minutes. Add a little hot liquid to egg yolks. Stir into mixture in pan. Cook for 1 minute. Remove from heat. Add butter, vanilla and coconut. Pour into baked pie shells. Cover with plastic wrap and chill. Top with whipped topping when serving. Makes 2 pies.

---

Submitted by:

Inn on the Square
3 Montgomery
Oakland, IL 61943
(217) 346-2289
Gary & Linda Miller
$45.00 (sgl.) to $50.00 (dbl.)

Full breakfast
3 rooms, 3 private baths
Children allowed
No pets
Restricted smoking
Mastercard & Visa

Offering warm hospitality and simple country pleasures, as well as historical sites, recreational activities, shopping excursions, and plain old "sittin' and rockin'." Relax in the Library, wander our "forest" out back, golf, swim, or visit Walnut Point, a beautiful conservation park. Near Lincoln Log Cabin State Park and an Amish settlement, too!

# COFFEE SHORTIES

**1 cup flour**
**1/2 cup cornstarch**
**1/2 cup powdered sugar**
**2 tablespoons dry instant coffee crystals, crushed**
**1 cup butter, softened**
**1/2 teaspoon vanilla**

Sift flour. Measure, then sift all dry ingredients together. Add softened butter. Cream until well-blended. Mix in vanilla. Refrigerate 2 hours. Pinch small pieces (1 teaspoon) and roll into balls. Flatten slightly with floured fork. Bake at 300° for 20 minutes. Makes 4 dozen cookies.

---

Submitted by:

Park Avenue Guest House
208 Park Avenue
Galena, IL 61036
(800) 359-0743
John & Sharon Fallbacher
$65.00 to $95.00

Continental plus breakfast
4 rooms, 4 private baths
Children, over 12
No pets
Restricted smoking
Mastercard, Visa & Discover

1893 Queen Anne Victorian "Painted Lady." Three rooms and one suite within walking distance of downtown shopping and restaurants. Gardens with gazebo. Screened wraparound porch. Antique furniture and decor.

# DOC O'BANNION'S APPLE PIE FROM OXBOW B&B

**6 - 8 apples, peeled, cored & sliced very thin**
**1 cup sugar**
**4 tablespoons all-purpose flour**
**2 tablespoons cornstarch**
**1/4 cup cinnamon candies**
**1/2 teaspoon nutmeg**
**5 slices butter**

**Pastry for 9" pie with top & bottom crusts**

Roll pie crust very thin. Roll on aluminum foil so it can be flipped into pan and onto pie. Fill bottom pie crust with apples. Cover apples with a mixture of sugar, flour, cornstarch, cinnamon candies, and nutmeg, and top with butter. Place top crust on pie. Cut slits in top. Bake at 400° for 50 - 60 minutes, depending on ripeness of apples. Makes 6 - 8 slices of pie.

---

Submitted by:

Oxbow Bed & Breakfast
Route 1, Box 47
Pinckneyville, IL 62274
(618) 357-9839
Dr. Al & Peggy Doughty
$50.00

Full breakfast
6 rooms, 6 private baths
Children, over 6
Vet. Hospital & Kennel next door
Restricted smoking
Mastercard & Visa

A 6,900 sq. ft. B&B on 3 levels, with Civil War decor and antique furniture, on ten acres of land. Honeymoon apartment in a restored barn. 2 rooms feature 4-poster canopy beds made from aged barn timbers. Woodworking shop, Arabian horses, excellent trails for walking or jogging.

# EASY FRUIT COBBLER

**1/2 cup butter, melted**
**3/4 cup flour**
**2 teaspoons baking powder**
**1 cup sugar**
**Pinch of salt**
**3/4 cup milk**
**2 cups chopped fruit, fresh or canned, any variety**

Melt butter in 8" x 8" pan. In bowl mix together all dry ingredients. Add milk to dry ingredients. Pour batter over melted butter in pan, but do not stir together. Place 2 cups chopped fruit on top of batter. Bake at 350° for 30 - 40 minutes, until golden brown. Serve warm. Makes 6 servings.

---

Submitted by:

Fannie's House
300 North Front Street
Danforth, IL 60930
(815) 269-2145
Don & Mary Noonan
$50.00 to $60.00

Continental plus breakfast
2 rooms, 2 private baths
Children, over 8
No pets
No smoking

100 year old home in peaceful country town, furnished in simple early 1900's period. Maps provided for bicycling, running or walking well-marked country roads. Overtired guests can call us for a pickup truck ride back to Fannie's, where lemonade and cookies will be waiting.

# LEMON ANGEL ROLL

**14 1/2 - 16 oz. pkg. Angel Food cake mix**
**Confectioner's sugar**
**14 oz. can Eagle Brand sweetened condensed milk**
**1/3 cup lemon juice**
**2 teaspoons lemon rind**
**4 - 6 drops yellow food coloring**
**4 oz. container frozen whipped topping (thawed)**
**1 cup flaked coconut (tinted yellow)**

Preheat oven to 350°. Line a 15" x 10" cookie sheet with aluminum foil, extending foil 1" over ends & sides. Prepare cake according to directions. Spread batter evenly over prepared cookie sheet. Bake 30 minutes or until top springs back when lightly touched. Immediately turn onto towel sprinkled with confectioner's sugar. Peel off foil. Beginning at narrow end, roll up jelly roll style. Cool thoroughly. Meanwhile in medium bowl, combine Eagle Brand milk, lemon juice and rind, and food coloring. Mix well. Fold in whipped topping. Unroll cooled cake carefully. Trim edges. Spread with half of lemon filling. Reroll. Place on serving plate seam side down. Spread with remaining filling. Garnish with tinted coconut. Chill at least 6 hours. Serves 12 - 16.

---

Submitted by:

Tiara Manor
403 W. Court St.
Paris, IL 61944
(800) 531-1865 or
In IL (217) 465-1865
Jo Marie & Rich Nowarita
$75.00 to $125.00

Full breakfast
4 rooms, 2 private baths
Children, over 12
No pets
No smoking
Mastercard & Visa

Luxuriate in the largest Gothic mansion in downstate IL, restored and decorated to the Civil War Period. 7 fireplaces, 20 chandeliers, with museum quality antiques throughout. Oak & walnut ribbon parquet floors, period wallpapers & floor coverings, Tea Room, and fine collectibles shop. 18' gazebo in a formal Victorian garden.

# MILLION DOLLAR DESSERT

**1 box Jiffy yellow cake mix**
**8 oz. cream cheese**
**1 pkg. instant vanilla pudding**
**2 cups milk (divided)**
**1 can pie filling (any flavor)**
**1 container Cool Whip**

Mix cake mix as directed. Put into 9" x 13" pan. Bake for 12 to 15 minutes at 350°. Let cool. Combine cream cheese with 1/2 cup milk. Mix pudding with remaining 1 1/2 cups milk, then mix together with cream cheese mixture. Spread on cake and let set. Cover with pie filling. Serve topped with Cool Whip. Makes 12 - 15 servings.

---

Submitted by:

Hart of Wenona
303 N. Walnut
Wenona, IL 61377
(815) 853-4778
Henry & Beverly Hart
$40.00

Continental plus breakfast
3 rooms
Children, over 10
No pets
No smoking

Turn-of-the-century house in a small town in central Illinois, features lovely stained glass, golden oak woodwork, a large verandah, and period antiques, with a/c. Relax and enjoy the elegance and charm of the past. Facilities available for rental for meetings, seminars, bridal showers, and special occasions.

# PECAN OR ENGLISH WALNUT PIE

**Pie crust:**
**1 cup flour**
**1/3 cup shortening**
**Cold water**

**Pie filling:**
**1/3 cup butter or margarine**
**3/4 cup brown sugar**
**3 eggs**
**1/2 cup light corn syrup**
**1/2 cup dark corn syrup**
**Dash of salt**
**1 teaspoon vanilla**
**1 cup pecans or English walnuts**

Cream butter until light. Add brown sugar and continue to cream. Add eggs one at a time beating after each addition. Add remainder of ingredients in order. Place in unbaked single pie crust. Bake at 375° for 40 - 50 minutes until golden brown and set. Makes 6 - 8 servings.

---

Submitted by:

Plymouth Rock Roost
201 W. Summer
Plymouth, IL 62637
(309) 458-6444
Ben Gentry & Joyce Steiner
$35.00 (sgl.) to $39.00 (dbl.)

Full breakfast
3 rooms, 2 shared baths
Children, over 12
No pets
No smoking
Mastercard & Visa

Spacious Queen Anne Victorian located in historic Hancock County is filled with antiques. Choice of Victorian Splendor, Country Charm or Family Heirloom oak rooms. Guests are welcome to use the whole house and join in antique related pastimes. Visit historic sites, golf, or just relax.

# PINEAPPLE CREAM CAKE

**2 cups sugar**
**2 cups flour**
**2 teaspoons baking soda**
**1 cup chopped nuts**
**20 oz. can crushed pineapple**
**2 eggs**

**Icing:**
**2 cups powdered sugar**
**8 oz. pkg. cream cheese**
**1 teaspoon vanilla**
**1 stick margarine**

Mix all ingredients together well. Grease and flour a 9" x 13" baking pan. Pour cake mixture into pan. Bake at 325° for 45 minutes. Mix icing ingredients together with mixer. Spread on hot cake. Can be frozen and served within six weeks. Makes 9 - 12 servings.

---

Submitted by:

Country Haus B&B
1191 Franklin
Carlyle, IL 62231
(618) 594-8313
Ron & Vickie Cook
$45.00 to $55.00

Full breakfast
4 rooms, 4 private baths
Children, over 3
No pets
No smoking
Mastercard, Visa, Am Ex

Located one mile from Carlyle Lake, Illinois' largest man-made lake. Swimming, fishing, boating, sailing, and skiing are a few of the activities you can enjoy. Originally built in the 1890's, you will find stained glass windows, pocket doors, a library with TV, and a jacuzzi.

# RED VELVET CAKE - A SOUTHERN SURPRISE IN THE NORTH

**Cake:**
**1 1/2 cups vegetable oil**
**1 1/2 cups granulated sugar**
**1 cup buttermilk**
**2 teaspoons vanilla extract**
**1 teaspoon baking soda**
**2 eggs**
**2 1/2 cups self-rising flour**

**Frosting:**
**8 oz. cream cheese**
**4 tablespoons butter**
**1 tablespoon milk**
**2 teaspoons vanilla extract**
**1 lb. box powdered sugar**
**1 1/2 cups chopped pecans**

Combine all cake ingredients except flour. Sift in flour. Beat for 3 - 5 minutes. Pour batter into 3 - 9" round cake pans. Bake at 350° for 25 - 30 minutes. Let cool. For frosting: Combine cream cheese and butter. Blend in milk and vanilla, then powdered sugar. Add pecans to cheese mixture, and frost cake. Enjoy! Makes 18 - 20 servings.

---

Submitted by:

Oscar Swan Country Inn
1800 West State Street
Geneva, IL 60134
(708) 232-0173
Hans & Nina Heymann
$70.00 to $135.00

Full breakfast
8 rooms, 4 private baths
Children allowed
Pets allowed
Restricted smoking
Mastercard, Visa, Am Ex

Beautiful gardens on 7 acres with outdoor pool. Garden Room with glassed 15-foot wall. Breakfast features homemade cinnamon bread, French toast, and country ham. Geneva is a special city with historic houses and boutiques. Bike paths follow the Fox River.

# RHUBARB PIE

**Pastry for 9" double crust pie**
**1 1/3 cups sugar**
**1/3 cup all-purpose flour**
**1/2 teaspoon grated orange peel (opt.)**
**2 cups rhubarb, cut into 1/2" pieces**
**2 cups sliced strawberries**
**2 tablespoons margarine or butter**
**1/4 teaspoon cinnamon**

Heat oven to 425°. Prepare pastry. Mix sugar, flour, and orange peel. Toss rhubarb and strawberries together. Turn half of the rhubarb mixture into pastry-lined pie plate. Sprinkle with half of sugar mixture. Repeat with remaining rhubarb and sugar mixtures. Dot with margarine. Cover with top crust that has slits cut in it. Sprinkle with cinnamon and a little extra sugar if desired. Cover edge of pie with 2" - 3" strip of aluminum foil to prevent excessive browning. Remove foil during last 15 minutes of baking. Bake until crust is brown, and juice begins to bubble through slits in crust, 40 - 50 minutes. This is our most requested recipe.

---

Submitted by:

La Maison du Rocher
Country Inn
#2 Duclos & Main, Box 163
Prairie du Rocher, IL 62277
(618) 284-3463
Jan Kennedy
$55.00 to $85.00
Ask about cottage rates

Full breakfast
3 rooms, 3 private baths
Children allowed only in cottage
No pets
Restricted smoking
Mastercard & Visa

Serving breakfast, lunch and dinner in an elegant country setting. Homemade cooking just like Grandma's: French white bread, whole wheat, kaiser rolls, fruit and cream pies, all baked daily. Daily entrée specials. Gift boutique. Rooms decorated in French Victorian style.

# SALLY'S BEST WALNUT RAISIN OATMEAL COOKIES

**1 cup butter**
**1/4 cup olive oil**
**3/4 cup brown sugar**
**1/2 cup granulated sugar**
**1 egg**
**1 teaspoon vanilla**
**1 1/4 cups whole wheat flour**
**1 teaspoon baking soda**
**1 teaspoon salt (opt.)**
**1 teaspoon cinnamon**
**1 cup raisins**
**1 cup walnuts**
**3 cups Quaker old-fashioned oats**

Heat oven to 375°. Beat butter, oil, and sugars. Beat in egg and vanilla. Combine flour, baking soda, salt and cinnamon. Add to liquid. Mix well. Add raisins, nuts and oats. Drop by rounded spoonfuls onto ungreased cookie sheet. Bake 12 minutes. Makes 4 dozen cookies.

---

Submitted by:

Chateau des Fleurs
552 Ridge Road
Winnetka, IL 60093
(708) 256-7272
Sally H. Ward
$80.00 (sgl.) to $90.00 (dbl.)

Full breakfast
3 rooms, 3 private baths
Children, over 11
No pets
No smoking
Mastercard & Visa

Authentic 1935 French country home, on 3/4 acre filled with magnificent trees, expansive lawns and English gardens. Exquisite view of terraced yard from 20' x 40' swimming pool. Filled with antiques, an elegant respite from the world welcoming you with light beauty, warmth and lovely views from every window.

# SOUTHERN ILLINOIS WHITE PIE

**1 1/2 cups milk**
**3/4 cup sugar**
**1/2 cup flour**
**3 teaspoons butter**
**1/2 teaspoon salt**
**1 teaspoon vanilla**
**2 egg whites**
**1/4 cup sugar**
**Baked 9" pie shell**
**1/2 pint whipping cream**
**1 or 2 teaspoons sugar**
**1/4 cup chopped pecans**

Mix first six ingredients in large saucepan. Cook and stir over medium heat until thickened. Remove from heat and set aside to cool. Beat 2 egg whites until stiff. Add 1/4 cup sugar, beat until well-blended. Fold into cooled pudding mixture. Pour into baked pie shell. Whip whipping cream. Add 1 or 2 teaspoons sugar and whip. Spread over top of pie in shell, sprinkle with pecans. Makes 8 "serendipelicious" servings!

---

Submitted by:

SugarWood -
The Inn at Chester
217 E. Buena Vista
Chester, IL 62233
(618) 826-2555
Betty Barnes-Hihn
$45.00 to $75.00

Full breakfast
4 rooms, 4 private baths
Children allowed
No pets
Restricted smoking
Mastercard & Visa

Delightful inn (circa 1910) offers all the romance and charm of the turn of the century. Named for its many hard maples, inn sits on a bluff above the Mississippi and looks to the Ozark Mountains. Guest rooms feature sitting area, antique furniture, & elegant appointments.

# SUMMER CHEESECAKE

**Crust:**
**3 cups graham cracker crumbs**
**1 stick soft butter**
**1/2 cup sugar**

**Filling:**
**1 can Milnot, chilled**
**1 pkg. lemon Jello**
**1 cup boiling water**
**1/2 cup sugar**
**8 oz. cream cheese**

Mix crust ingredients, and press into 9" x 13" pan. Bake 8 minutes at 350°. Chill Milnot, then whip. Dissolve Jello in 1 cup boiling water, cool, and add to Milnot. Blend in softened cream cheese. Pour over crust and chill at least one hour.

---

Submitted by:

The Poor Farm
R.R. #3
Mt. Carmel, IL 62863
(618) 262-4663
Liz & John Stelzer
$30.00 to $50.00

Full breakfast
5 rooms
Children allowed
Pets by prior arrangement only
Restricted smoking

In simpler times, this 1915, 30 room structure served as home for the homeless. Today, it's home for the traveler enjoying country charm, local history and old-time hospitality. Historic Mt. Carmel, on the banks of the Wabash, offers one of the state's finest 18-hole golf courses. Beall Woods State Park is a leisurely 15-minute drive.

# WHITE CHOCOLATE CHEESECAKE

**Crust:**
**1 cup crushed chocolate cookie wafers**
**2 tablespoons melted margarine**

**Topping:**
**1 cup sliced fresh strawberries**
**1 kiwi, peeled and sliced**

**Filling:**
**1 envelope unflavored gelatin**
**1/2 cup water**
**1/2 cup sugar**
**8 oz. softened cream cheese**
**1 cup sour cream**
**6 oz. white baking chocolate, melted**
**1 cup whipping cream**
**1/2 teaspoon vanilla**

Combine crust ingredients. Mix well. Press in the bottom of springform pan. Set aside. In small saucepan combine gelatin and water. Let stand 1 minute. Add sugar, stir over medium heat until mixture is dissolved. In large bowl, beat cream cheese and sour cream until creamy. Gradually add melted chocolate, gelatin mixture, whipping cream and vanilla. Beat until smooth. Pour into crust. Cover and refrigerate 1 1/2 to 2 1/2 hours or until firm. Shortly before serving run a knife around edge of pan to loosen cheesecake. Carefully remove form sides of pan. Arrange fruit over cheesecake. Store in refrigerator. Makes 16 servings.

---

Submitted by:

Corner George Inn
Corner of Main & Mill
Maeystown, IL 62256
(618) 458-6660
David & Marcia Braswell
$65.00 to $95.00

Full breakfast
5 rooms, 5 private baths
Children, over 12
No pets
No smoking
Mastercard & Visa

The inn and Maeystown General Store, built in 1884, are in historic Maeystown, about 45 minutes southeast of St. Louis. Antique-filled guest rooms, 2 sitting rooms, and a ballroom. Bicycles & horse-drawn carriages available. Experience the German flavor of a bygone era.

# TOUR ILLINOIS

# TOUR ILLINOIS

The Illinois Bed & Breakfast Association (IBBA) would like to introduce you to the abundance of Illinois. Illinois is divided into four Tourism Regions. The IBBA has further divided Northern Region into Northeast and Northwest. Each region is represented on the following pages. Discover the diversity of Illinois in these pages. Wherever you travel in Illinois you will find an IBBA member inn close by.

Not all IBBA members chose to participate in this book, however, all towns listed on the map on page 103 do host IBBA member inns. For a complete guide of member B&B's, please write:

Illinois Bed & Breakfast Association
P.O. Box 823
Monmouth, IL 61462

## A Word About Quality

In an effort to assure the Bed & Breakfast traveller a pleasant stay at all member B&B's, the Illinois Bed & Breakfast Association has begun to review all of our members. We are evaluating our inns for cleanliness, hospitality and safety. This process has just begun, so all of the B&B's included in this book have not necessarily been reviewed by our Quality Assurance Reviewers. We welcome your comments concerning any of our member inns. We are dedicated to quality and will continue to do everything in our power to assure you a wonderful stay at our Bed & Breakfasts.

# SOUTHERN REGION

The Southern Region of Illinois, featuring 35 counties, is well known for its outdoor life, but each section of the region is rich in its own way.

The Northwest section of the Southern region is located within an hour's drive of downtown St. Louis. You'll find archaeological discoveries at Cahokia Mounds, great antique shopping in Alton, B&B's from Elsah to Maeystown and great fishing and boating at Carlyle Lake.

The Northeast section of the region is known for its fishing as well as its historic sites, great food and several antique and unique gift shops.

Shawnee National Forest stretches across the Southern region of Illinois from the Ohio River to the Mississippi. There are hiking, fishing and hunting facilities, as well as parks, refuge areas and interpretive centers throughout the nearly quarter of a million acres of forest.

The Cache River Wetlands are in the Southwest section of the Southern region. This area is the home of thousand-year-old cypress trees and many plants and animals threatened with extinction. Here you can view and learn about the wetland area.

The Smithland Dam in the Southeast section was built in 1980. It elevates the Ohio River pool by 15 feet. This has created a 23,000 acre fishery for bluegill, crappie, catfish, bass and sauger.

Whether you want to get back to nature, visit historic sites or go antiquing, the Southern Region is for you.

Southern Illinois Tourism Council
Route 1, P.O. Box 40
Whittington, IL 62897
(618) 629-2506 or (800) 342-3100

## NORTHEAST REGION

The Northeast region of Illinois is ladled with some of the world's best shopping, antiques galore, outdoor recreation second to none, and cultural history.

Shoppers can get lost in dozens of malls such as Woodfield Mall in Schaumburg or the Gurnee Mills Outlet Mall in Gurnee (the largest outlet mall in the world). If shopping for something old is more your style, the Fox River Valley is the place to be. St. Charles is home to the Kane County Flea Market with over 1,000 dealers every month. Or "shop 'till you drop" in town at one of the many quaint, antique stores. And don't forget to stop in Geneva, Batavia, Richmond, and Ridgefield . . . all brimming with quality antiques and shops.

The outdoor recreation activities along the I&M Canal National Heritage Corridor are unlimited. Along the canal you'll find fourteen state parks, fish and wildlife conservation areas offering fishing, hiking, nature preserves, canyons and waterfalls. The cultural history of the area during the French-Indian fur trade era can be found at the Isle A La Cache Museum in Romeoville. Or, stop by the Brandon Lock & Dam in Joliet to see how the lock and dam facilities operate on the rivers.

Northern Illinois. Don't Miss It!

Northern Illinois Tourism Council
150 N. 9th Street
Rockford, IL 61107
(815) 964-6482 or (800) 248-6482

## NORTHWEST REGION

In the northwest corner of the state you'll find the Mighty Mississippi, quality antiques, charming bed and breakfast inns, scenic vistas and fine museums.

Antique buffs will not want to miss Galena. . . over 100 antique shops and stores intertwined with some of the most beautiful scenery in Illinois. Here you'll find that Illinois is definitely not flat! The rolling hills and bluffs of the Mississippi River are also home to the great bald eagle. Carroll and Whiteside county offer many areas to stop and catch a glimpse of this fascinating bird. Travel east a bit to Rockford to see one of the world's finest and most extensive collections of time-keeping devices at the Time Museum. Or maybe you'd rather get your feet wet at Magic Waters, one of the largest wave pools in Illinois.

History nuts can have fun visiting the homes of Ulysses S. Grant in Galena or Ronald Reagan in Dixon. Or stop in at the Ellwood House Museum, former home of Isaac Ellwood, the co-inventor of barbed wire.

Northern Illinois. Don't Miss It!

Northern Illinois Tourism Council
150 N. 9th Street
Rockford, IL 61107
(815) 964-6482 or (800) 248-6482

## WESTERN REGION

Western Illinois boasts 20 counties with the Mississippi River as its western boundary and the Illinois River to its east.

Many Western Illinois cities were brought forth because of the rivers. The oldest European settlement in Illinois can be found in Western Illinois. Also born of the river, Western Illinois is home to riverboat gambling. Non-gaming riverboats are also available for cruising.

The rivers also provide many beautiful hiking and biking trails. The area has many lakes and parks where outdoor activities can be enjoyed. For the golf enthusiast, golf courses abound.

Western Illinois offers an historic Mormon settlement on the Mississippi River where many historical homes and shops are open to visitors. Old-time crafts have been revitalized and daily demonstrations are given by skilled artisans.

In Western Illinois you can also find a Swedish community dating back to 1846. Here a visitor may enjoy one of the many Swedish festivals highlighting delicious Swedish and American foods, museums, tours and crafts.

Western Illinois hosts many fairs and festivals with each event heralding its own specialty.

Education is also an important part of Western Illinois with 17 institutions of higher education.

The symbol of America, the bald eagle, has several winter roosting places in Western Illinois.

Western Illinois offers many shopping meccas where you can find merchandise for yourself or your home. For a different kind of shopping trip, try the highways and byways of Western Illinois. You will find a multitude of antique and specialty shops.

We invite you to travel any of the five very popular scenic drives located in Western Illinois and see what we have to offer.

Western Illinois Tourism Council
107 E. Carroll
Macomb, IL 61455
(309) 837-7460 or (800) 232-3889

# CENTRAL REGION

From the Indiana border on the East to the banks of the Illinois River on the West, Central Illinois abounds with historic and family places and recreational opportunities.

Only in Central Illinois can you trace the life of Abraham Lincoln as he grew to be a mature legislator, married, and later became the 16th President of the United States.

Don't miss the opportunity to explore our fascinating past at any of the eleven historical sites located in Central Illinois. History you can see and actually feel and experience is found here.

While Central Illinois is known for it's Lincoln sites, it is also the location of the Dana Thomas House, one of the masterpieces of Frank Lloyd Wright. The home is designed in the early prairie-style and furnished with original Wright-designed pieces.

Central Illinois is the seat of the Illinois state government with Springfield serving as our capital. Central Illinois is also home for many nationally known institutions of higher education.

Illinois' only Amish Community is located in the heart of Central Illinois, offering a close look at a simple lifestyle that has endured the changes in modern times. Amish horse and buggies still travel the streets.

Each year Central Illinois hosts hundreds of fairs and festivals. The Illinois State Fair, one of the nation's largest agricultural fairs, is held every August in Springfield.

If you are an outdoor enthusiast, Central Illinois has fishing and outdoor recreation activities for everyone.

Drive the city streets or country roads and discover the antique and collectible shops which will both surprise and delight young and old alike.

Come visit Central Illinois.

Central Illinois Tourism Council
629 E. Washington
Springfield, IL 62701
(217) 525-7980 or (800) 262-2482

# ILLINOIS MAP

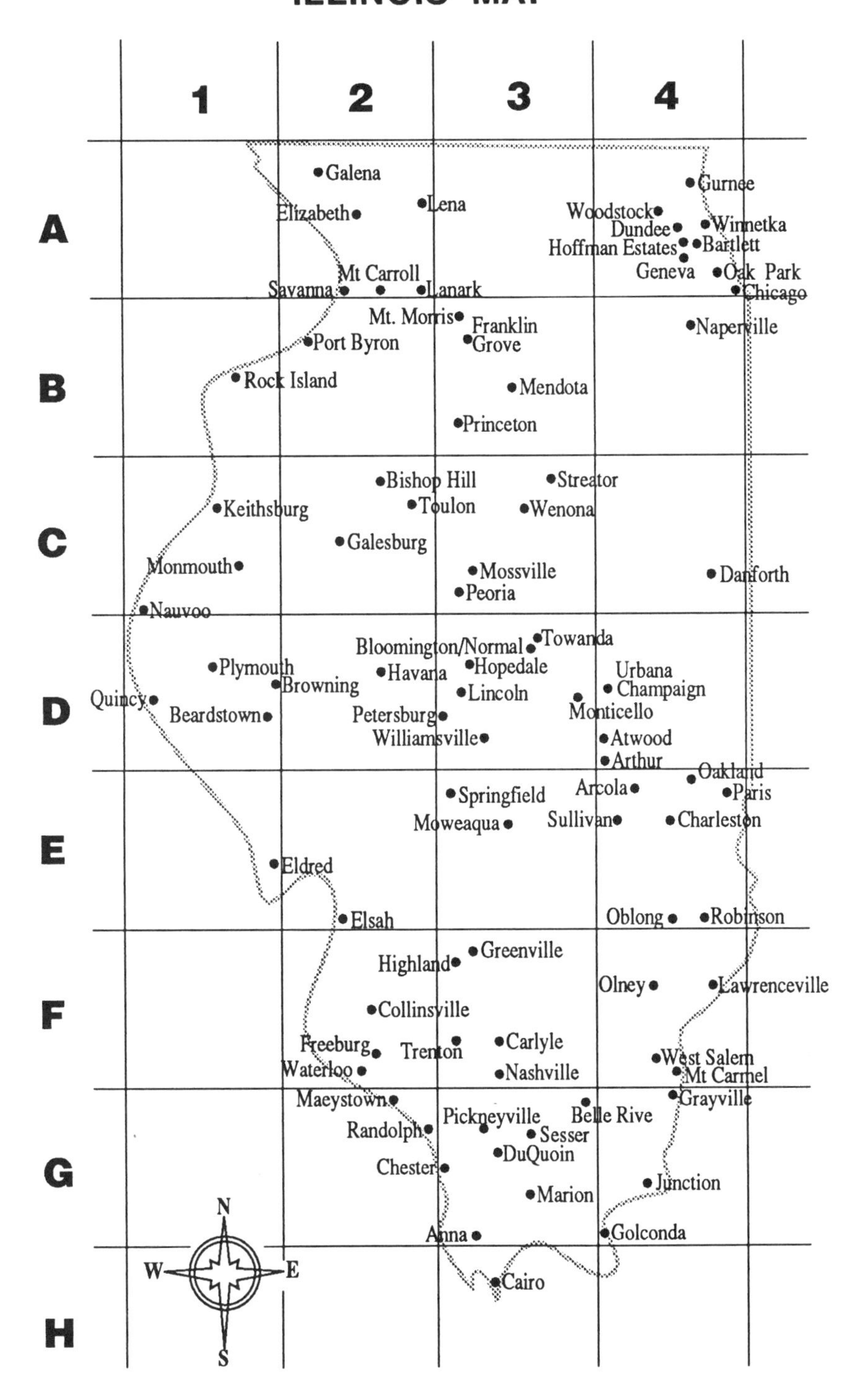

## INDEX OF BED & BREAKFASTS

# NOTES

# NOTES

# NOTES

# NOTES

# NOTES

# ORDER FORMS

---

## *Inn-describably Delicious*

I would like to order *Inn-describably Delicious, Recipes From The Illinois Bed and Breakfast Association Innkeepers.* I have indicated the quantity below. MAIL THIS ORDER TO: Winters Publishing, P.O. Box 501, Greensburg, IN 47240.

_____ *Inn-describably Delicious* $9.95 each ___________

Shipping Charge $2.00 each ___________

Sales Tax ( Indiana residents ONLY ) $ .60 each ___________

TOTAL ___________

Please send to:

Name: ______________________________

Address: ______________________________

City: ______________ State: __________ Zip: __________

---

## *Inn-describably Delicious*

I would like to order *Inn-describably Delicious, Recipes From The Illinois Bed and Breakfast Association Innkeepers.* I have indicated the quantity below. MAIL THIS ORDER TO: Winters Publishing, P.O. Box 501, Greensburg, IN 47240.

_____ *Inn-describably Delicious* $9.95 each ___________

Shipping Charge $2.00 each ___________

Sales Tax ( Indiana residents ONLY ) $ .60 each ___________

TOTAL ___________

Please send to:

Name: ______________________________

Address: ______________________________

City: ______________ State: __________ Zip: __________

---

## *More B&B Cookbooks from Winters Publishing*

*The Indiana Bed & Breakfast Association Cookbok and Directory*
Features recipes from 75 inns throughout the state of Indiana, with complete information about each inn. 96 pgs. $9.95

*Overnight Sensations - Recipes From Virginia's Finest Bed & Breakfasts*
Features recipes from 90 inns throughout the state of Virginia, with complete information about each inn. 112 pgs. $9.95

*Pure Gold - Colorado Treasures, Recipes From Bed & Breakfast Innkeepers of Colorado*
Features more than 100 recipes from 54 inns throughout the state of Colorado, with complete information about each inn. 96 pgs. $9.95

*Just Inn Time for Breakfast - A Cookbook from the Michigan Lake To Lake Bed and Breakfast Association*
Features recipes from 93 inns throughout the state of Michigan, with complete information about each inn. 128 pgs. $10.95

*Breakfast Cookbook 2 - More Recipes From America's Bed & Breakfast Inns*
Features breakfast recipes from 300 inns throughout the country, with complete information about each inn. 320 pgs. $12.95

---

I have indicated the quantity of the book(s) that I wish to order below. MAIL THIS ORDER TO:

Winters Publishing, P.O. Box 501, Greensburg, IN 47240.

Qty.

_____ *Indiana B&B Assn. Cookbook* $ 9.95 each ___________

_____ *Overnight Sensations* $ 9.95 each ___________

_____ *Pure Gold - Colorado Treasures* $ 9.95 each ___________

_____ *Just Inn Time for Breakfast* $10.95 each ___________

_____ *Breakfast Cookbook 2* $12.95 each ___________

Shipping Charge $ 2.00 each ___________

5% Sales Tax ( Indiana residents ONLY ) ___________

TOTAL ___________

Please send to:

Name: ____________________

Address: ____________________

City: __________ State: __________ Zip: __________